Florian Fittkau

Simulating Cloud Deployment Options for Software Migration Support

Anchor Academic
Publishing

Fittkau, Florian: Simulating Cloud Deployment Options for Software Migration Support,
Hamburg, Anchor Academic Publishing 2015

Buch-ISBN: 978-3-95489-393-5
PDF-eBook-ISBN: 978-3-95636-352-8
Druck/Herstellung: Anchor Academic Publishing, Hamburg, 2015

Bibliografische Information der Deutschen Nationalbibliothek:
Die Deutsche Nationalbibliothek verzeichnet diese Publikation in der Deutschen
Nationalbibliografie; detaillierte bibliografische Daten sind im Internet über
http://dnb.d-nb.de abrufbar.

Bibliographical Information of the German National Library:
The German National Library lists this publication in the German National Bibliography.
Detailed bibliographic data can be found at: http://dnb.d-nb.de

All rights reserved. This publication may not be reproduced, stored in a retrieval system
or transmitted, in any form or by any means, electronic, mechanical, photocopying,
recording or otherwise, without the prior permission of the publishers.

Das Werk einschließlich aller seiner Teile ist urheberrechtlich geschützt. Jede Verwertung
außerhalb der Grenzen des Urheberrechtsgesetzes ist ohne Zustimmung des Verlages
unzulässig und strafbar. Dies gilt insbesondere für Vervielfältigungen, Übersetzungen,
Mikroverfilmungen und die Einspeicherung und Bearbeitung in elektronischen Systemen.

Die Wiedergabe von Gebrauchsnamen, Handelsnamen, Warenbezeichnungen usw. in
diesem Werk berechtigt auch ohne besondere Kennzeichnung nicht zu der Annahme,
dass solche Namen im Sinne der Warenzeichen- und Markenschutz-Gesetzgebung als frei
zu betrachten wären und daher von jedermann benutzt werden dürften.

Die Informationen in diesem Werk wurden mit Sorgfalt erarbeitet. Dennoch können
Fehler nicht vollständig ausgeschlossen werden und die Diplomica Verlag GmbH, die
Autoren oder Übersetzer übernehmen keine juristische Verantwortung oder irgendeine
Haftung für evtl. verbliebene fehlerhafte Angaben und deren Folgen.

Alle Rechte vorbehalten

© Anchor Academic Publishing, Imprint der Diplomica Verlag GmbH
Hermannstal 119k, 22119 Hamburg
http://www.diplomica-verlag.de, Hamburg 2015
Printed in Germany

Abstract

Cloud computing is emerging as a promising new paradigm that aims at delivering computing resources and services on demand. To cope with the frequently found over- and under-provisioning of resources in conventional data centers, cloud computing technologies enable to rapidly scale up and down according to varying workload patterns. However, most software systems are not built for utilizing this so called elasticity and therefore must be adapted during the migration process into the cloud. A challenge during migration is the high number of different possibilities for the deployment to cloud computing resources. For example, there exist a plethora of potential cloud provider candidates. Here, the selection of a specific cloud provider is the most obvious and basic cloud deployment option. Furthermore, the mapping between services and virtual machine instances must be considered when migrating to the cloud and the specific adaptation strategies, like allocating a new virtual machine instance if the CPU utilization is above a given threshold, have to be chosen and configured. The set of combinations of the given choices form a huge design space which is infeasible to test manually. Simulating the different deployment options assists to find the best ratio between high performance and low costs.

For this purpose, we developed a simulation tool named CDOSim that can simulate those cloud deployment options. CDOSim integrates into the cloud migration framework CloudMIG Xpress and utilizes KDM models that were extracted by a reverse engineering process. Furthermore, it is possible to use monitored workload profiles as a simulation input. Our evaluation shows that CDOSim's simulation results can support software engineers to sufficiently accurate predict the cost and performance properties of software systems when deployed to private and real world public cloud environments such as Eucalyptus and Amazon EC2, respectively. Thus, CDOSim can be used for the simulation of cloud deployment options and assists to find the best suited cloud deployment option for existing software systems.

Contents

1	**Introduction**	**1**
	1.1 Motivation	1
	1.2 Approach	1
	1.3 Goals	3
	1.4 Document Structure	4
2	**Foundations and Technologies**	**5**
	2.1 Foundations	5
	2.2 Involved Technologies	12
3	**Simulation Input**	**21**
	3.1 Overview	21
	3.2 MIPIPS	22
	3.3 Instruction Count	27
	3.4 Weights per Statement	40
	3.5 Network Traffic	41
	3.6 SMM Workload Profile	43
	3.7 Enriched KDM Model	43
	3.8 Adaptation Rules	44
	3.9 Configuration	44
4	**Simulation Output**	**47**
	4.1 Costs	47
	4.2 Response Times	47
	4.3 SLA Violations	47
	4.4 Rating	48
5	**CloudSim Enhancements**	**49**
	5.1 Overview	49
	5.2 Enhanced CloudSim Meta-Model	49
	5.3 CPU Utilization Model per Core	51

5.4	Starting and Stopping Virtual Machine Instances on Demand	51
5.5	Delayed Cloudlet Creation	52
5.6	Delayed Start of Virtual Machines	52
5.7	Timeout for Cloudlets	52
5.8	Improved Debt Model	53
5.9	Enhanced Instruction Count Model	53
5.10	History Exporter	53
5.11	Dynamic Host Addition at Runtime	54
5.12	Method Calls and Network Traffic between Virtual Machine Instances	54

6 MIPIPS and Weights Benchmark   57
- 6.1 Features . . . 57
- 6.2 Design . . . 57
- 6.3 Example Output . . . 59

7 CDOSim   61
- 7.1 Features . . . 61
- 7.2 The Simulation Process . . . 62
- 7.3 Design . . . 63

8 Evaluation of CDOSim   65
- 8.1 Goals of the Evaluation . . . 65
- 8.2 Methodology . . . 66
- 8.3 Basic Experiment Setup . . . 67
- 8.4 E1: MIPIPS Benchmark Evaluation . . . 74
- 8.5 E2: Accuracy Evaluation for Single Core Instances . . . 80
- 8.6 E3: Accuracy Evaluation for Multi Core Instances . . . 99
- 8.7 E4: Accuracy Evaluation for Adaptation Strategy Configurations . . . 104
- 8.8 E5: Inter-Cloud Accuracy Evaluation . . . 109
- 8.9 Summary . . . 112

9 Related Work   115
- 9.1 GroudSim . . . 115
- 9.2 Palladio . . . 115
- 9.3 SLAstic.SIM . . . 115
- 9.4 iCanCloud . . . 116
- 9.5 Byte Instruction Count for Java . . . 116

9.6	Measuring Elasticity	117
9.7	Dhrystone Benchmark	117
9.8	Cloudstone Toolkit	118

10 Conclusions and Future Work   **119**
    10.1 Conclusions 119
    10.2 Future Work 119

References   **121**

A Glossary   **i**

B Ecore Model for MIPIPS and Weights Benchmark   **iii**

C KDM example   **v**

D Rating Algorithm   **xi**

E Attachments   **xv**

List of Figures

1	Users and providers of cloud computing taken from Armbrust et al. [2]	8
2	CloudMIG approach taken from Frey et al. [19]	10
3	CloudSim architecture taken from Calheiros et al. [10]	13
4	CloudMIG Xpress overview taken from Frey et al. [19]	14
5	Extracted CloudSim meta-model	15
6	Layers of KDM taken from Pérez-Castillo et al. [54]	16
7	Example of determining the median of response times during phases of low CPU utilization in the dynamic approach	30
8	Enhanced CloudSim meta-model	50
9	CPU utilization model example	52
10	New scheduling example	55
11	Java packages of the MIPIPS and weights benchmark	58
12	GUI of the MIPIPS and weights benchmark	58
13	Activities in CDOSim's simulation process	62
14	Java packages of CDOSim	63
15	GUI of CDOSim	64
16	Deployment configuration for Eucalyptus	70
17	Deployment configuration for Amazon EC2	72
18	The used day-night-cycle workload intensity	73
19	Average CPU utilization of allocated nodes in SingleCore.1 experiment	83
20	Median of response times in SingleCore.1 experiment	84
21	Average CPU utilization of allocated nodes in SingleCore.2 experiment	84
22	Median of response times in SingleCore.2 experiment	85
23	Average CPU utilization of allocated nodes in SingleCore.3 experiment	86
24	Median response times in SingleCore.3 experiment	87
25	Average CPU utilization of allocated nodes in SingleCore.4 experiment	87
26	Median response times in SingleCore.4 experiment	88
27	Average CPU utilization of allocated nodes in SingleCore.5 experiment	89
28	Median response times in SingleCore.5 experiment	90
29	Average CPU utilization of allocated nodes in SingleCore.6 experiment	91
30	Median response times in SingleCore.6 experiment	92
31	Average CPU utilization of allocated nodes in SingleCore.7 experiment	92
32	Median response times in SingleCore.7 experiment	93
33	Average CPU utilization of allocated nodes in SingleCore.8 experiment	94

34	Median response times in SingleCore.8 experiment	95
35	Average CPU utilization of allocated nodes in MultiCore.1 experiment	101
36	Median response times in MultiCore.1 experiment	101
37	Average CPU utilization of allocated nodes in MultiCore.2 experiment	102
38	Median response times in MultiCore.2 experiment	103
39	Average CPU utilization of allocated nodes in Adaptation.1 experiment	105
40	Median response times in Adaptation.1 experiment	106
41	Average CPU utilization of allocated nodes in Adaptation.2 experiment	107
42	Median response times in Adaptation.2 experiment	107
43	Average CPU utilization of allocated nodes in PredictionAmazon.1 experiment	110
44	Median response times in PredictionAmazon.1 experiment	111
45	Ecore model for MIPIPS and weights benchmark as UML class diagram	iii

List of Tables

1	Overview of the preconditions for each instruction count derivation approach	28
2	Example weights	37
3	Contained weight benchmarks	42
4	Simulation configuration parameters	44
5	Our Eucalyptus server	69
6	Our Eucalyptus configuration	69
7	Used instance types in Amazon EC2 experiments	71
8	Default simulation configuration	74
9	Results for comparison MIPIPS.1	76
10	Results for comparison MIPIPS.2	76
11	Results for comparison MIPIPS.3	77
12	Results for comparison MIPIPS.4	77
13	Results for comparison MIPIPS.5	78
14	Overview of the relative error values for each scenario	113

1 Introduction

1.1 Motivation

Cloud computing is emerging as a promising new paradigm that aims at delivering computing resources and services on demand. To cope with the frequently found over- and under-provisioning of resources in conventional data centers, cloud computing technologies enable to rapidly scale up and down according to varying workload patterns. However, most software systems are not built for utilizing this so called elasticity and therefore must be adapted during the migration process into the cloud [46].

Here, the selection of a specific cloud provider is the most obvious and basic cloud deployment option. Furthermore, the mapping between services and virtual machine instances must be considered when migrating to the cloud and the specific adaptation strategies, like allocating a new virtual machine instance if the CPU utilization is above a given threshold, have to be chosen and configured. The set of combinations of the given choices form a huge design space which is infeasible to test manually [25].

The simulation of a cloud deployment option can assist in solving this problem. A simulation is often faster than executing real world experiments. Furthermore, the adaptation to the software system, that shall be migrated, requires less effort at a modeling layer. The simulation can be utilized by an automatic optimization algorithm to find the best ratio between high performance and low costs.

1.2 Approach

We begin with defining the fundamental concept of a cloud deployment option and describe our simulation approach.

Definition 1 *In the context of a deployment of software on a cloud platform, a cloud deployment option is a combination of decisions concerning the selection of a cloud provider, the deployment of components to virtual machine instances, the virtual machine instances' configuration, and specific adaptation strategies.*

Definition 1 shows our definition of a cloud deployment option. The deployment of components to virtual machine instances includes the case that new components might be formed of parts of already existing components. By a virtual machine instances' configuration, we refer to the instance type, as m1.small in the case of Amazon EC2, of virtual machine instances, for instance. Furthermore, an example for an adaptation strategy is "start a new virtual machine instance when for 60 seconds the average CPU utilization of allocated nodes stays above 70 %."

For simulating a cloud deployment option, we basically need a cloud environment simulator. For this purpose, we utilize CloudSim [10]. There are various inputs that are required by CloudSim. For modeling a computation like an application call, named *Cloudlet* in CloudSim, CloudSim mainly requires the *instruction count* of the computation. The instruction count of a Cloudlet is a measure for the work that has to be conducted by the CPU. As a central input for modeling the capacity of virtual machine instances, CloudSim needs the mega instructions per second (MIPS) of the virtual machine instance. MIPS are a measure for the computing performance of the virtual machine instance. CloudSim does neither define a method for deriving the instruction count nor the MIPS. Furthermore, CloudSim does not specify which instructions are meant.

We assume that CloudSim requires instructions on a language level, e.g., *double divide* and *integer minus*, and that these instructions all equally flow into the MIPS value. Hence, we consider MIPS as too coarse grained because different instructions have different runtimes in general. Therefore, we define the measure mega integer plus instructions per second (MIPIPS). The measurement of MIPIPS should be separate from the actual simulation software because it has to be run on the virtual machine instances to measure their MIPIPS, for example. In accordance to MIPIPS, the instruction count unit of a Cloudlet has to be in integer plus instructions. Other instruction types must be converted to these integer plus instructions by weights that will also be measured separately from the actual simulation software.

To rate the suitability of a specific cloud deployment option, the simulation has to compute some information like costs for the given cloud deployment option. Furthermore, the outputs of a simulation run have to be comparable to the outputs of other simulation runs. This leads to the need for a rating approach.

A further requirement for the simulation results from the wide range of programming languages supported by different cloud providers. Infrastructure-as-a-Service (IaaS) providers typically support all programming languages because they are only providing the infrastructure computing resources. Therefore, we need a language independent simulation. For this purpose, we utilize the Knowledge Discovery Meta-Model (KDM) that provides information about the existing software system in a language independent way.

CloudMIG [15] provides a promising approach to assist in a migration project to a cloud environment. There also exists a prototype implementation, called CloudMIG Xpress [18], that implements this approach. Our software, named Cloud Deployment Options Simulator (CDOSim), for realizing the simulation contributes to CloudMIG Xpress as a plug-in. It utilizes workload profiles that can be modeled by the user or can be imported from monitoring data that were recorded by, for instance, Kieker [70].

1.3 Goals

Our main objective is a software that enables the simulation of cloud deployment options on a language independent basis. For this purpose, we define the following goals.

1.3.1 G1: Definition of the Simulation Input

The definition of the simulation input should be accomplished by goal G1. MIPIPS and instruction count was already described as an input. However, there are more. Furthermore, where appropriate, derivation methods for the input parameter should be developed or defined.

1.3.2 G2: Definition of the Simulation Output

In goal G2 the output of the simulation should be defined. Furthermore, a metric for comparing the cloud deployment options in respect to the output should be developed.

1.3.3 G3: Development of a Benchmark for Measuring the Computing Performance of a Node in MIPIPS

In G3 a benchmark for measuring the computing performance of a node in MIPIPS, that can be easily adapted to new programming languages, shall be developed. It shall include a GUI and a console interface because virtual machine instances can often only be accessed via a command shell.

1.3.4 G4: Development of CDOSim

The last goal is the development of a software that realizes the simulation. Furthermore, it shall be integrated into CloudMIG Xpress as a plug-in. We name this software CDOSim. To achieve the programming language independence, CDOSim shall operate on KDM instances.

1.4 Document Structure

The remainder of the thesis is structured as follows. Section 2 outlines the foundations and utilized technologies. Afterwards, Section 3 presents the simulation inputs and how they can be derived (G1). Then, Section 4 describes the simulation output (G2) and a rating approach for rating simulation runs relatively to each other. The enhancements we needed to conduct for CloudSim are listed in Section 5. The following Section 6 describes our MIPIPS and weights benchmark (G3). Our developed tool for simulating cloud deployment options, named CDOSim, is discussed in Section 7 (G4). The following Section 8 evaluates the functionality and accuracy of CDOSim. Then, Section 9 describes related work. The final Section 10 concludes the thesis and defines the future work.

2 Foundations and Technologies

Sections 2.1 to 2.2 provide an overview of the foundations and technologies that will be used in later sections.

2.1 Foundations

The following Sections 2.1.1 to 2.1.5 describe the foundations.

2.1.1 Cloud Computing

Cloud computing is a relatively new computing paradigm. Therefore, many definitions for cloud computing exist. Here, we use the National Institute of Standards and Technology (NIST) definition by Mell and Grance [42] because this definition has become a de-facto standard.

The NIST definition for cloud computing defines five essential characteristics that a service must fulfill in order to be a cloud service, for example, on-demand self-service. Furthermore, it describes three different service models. These are IaaS, Platform-as-a-Service (PaaS), and Software-as-a-Service (SaaS). They differ in the levels of abstraction with regard to configuration and programming options. Clouds can be deployed according to four different deployment models. These are public clouds, private clouds, hybrid clouds, and community clouds. In addition, Armbrust et al. [2] define different role models for users and providers of cloud computing services.

Essential Characteristics

The NIST definition for cloud computing defines five essential characteristics that a service must fulfill in order to be a cloud service. These are listed and described below.

1. On-demand self-service

A user can rent computing capabilities like storage and computing time on demand in an automatic way without human interaction of the service provider.

2. Broad network access

The capabilities can be accessed over the network by standard mechanisms. These standard mechanisms are available on heterogeneous platforms like mobile phones and laptops.

3. Resource pooling

The cloud provider's computing resources are pooled to serve multiple cloud users. The location, where the physical or virtual resources are allocated, is not exactly known by the cloud users.

4. Rapid elasticity

Virtually unlimited resources can be rapidly and elastically allocated to enable quick scale up and down. It can be purchased by the cloud users in any quantity at any time.

5. Measured Service

By monitoring the usage, the cloud system automatically controls and optimizes the used resources. For the cloud provider and cloud users, transparency is provided by monitoring, controlling, and reporting the resource usage data.

Service Models

The cloud providers can offer their service at different levels of abstraction with regard to configuration and programming options. The different kinds of service models are described in the following three paragraphs.

Infrastructure-as-a-Service (IaaS)

Infrastructure-as-a-Service provides the lowest level of abstraction with a maximum of configuration options compared to the other service models. In IaaS, the cloud user setups and runs instances of previously created or provided virtual machine images. Therefore, the cloud user can create the full software stack by himself. A popular cloud provider that offers IaaS is, for instance, Amazon with its Elastic Compute Cloud (EC2).

Platform-as-a-Service (PaaS)

Considering the PaaS model, the cloud provider defines and maintains the programming environment for the cloud user. Many PaaS providers only support specific programming languages with even more constraints to meet the environment specifications. Examples for PaaS providers are Google App Engine [21] and Microsoft Azure [45].

Software-as-a-Service (SaaS)

SaaS provides the highest level of abstraction with no configuration options apart from the rented software. The cloud user rents access to the software in the cloud. The cloud user advantages can be avoided installation and maintenance effort, for instance. Examples for SaaS-based products are Google Docs or Microsoft Office Live.

Deployment Models

Clouds can be deployed using four different deployment models. These are public clouds, private clouds, hybrid clouds, and community clouds. These deployment models are briefly outlined in the next four paragraphs.

Public Clouds

In a public cloud, the cloud infrastructure can be accessed by the general public. For instance, Amazon provides a public cloud named Amazon EC2.

Private Clouds

Public clouds can have disadvantages for some users. First, there might be legal aspects that prohibit to use public clouds for data protection reasons. Furthermore, cloud providers can go bankrupt. For avoiding those disadvantages, private cloud software can be deployed on the own servers. An example for a private cloud software is Eucalyptus.

Hybrid Clouds

In this deployment model, private and public cloud providers are used together by a cloud user. Companies often use this kind to combine the advantages of public and private clouds. The privacy-critical applications are executed in a private cloud and the rest of the applications are run in a public cloud.

Community Clouds

The last deployment model is a community cloud. This kind of a cloud provides access only to a special community.

Role Models

Armbrust et al. [2] define the role models *cloud provider, SaaS provider, cloud user,* and *SaaS user*. The associations between them is shown in Figure 1. A *cloud provider* offers the *cloud users* the resources in terms of utility computing. Thus, he provides the resources on an IaaS or PaaS service basis. A special kind of *cloud user* is a *SaaS providers*. The *SaaS provider* makes SaaS services available to *SaaS users* through web applications. The NIST defines similar role models [41].

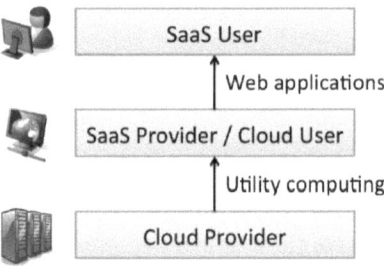

Figure 1: Users and providers of cloud computing taken from Armbrust et al. [2]

2.1.2 Software Modernization

Jha and Maheshwari [32] propose a classification of current modernization approaches. They identified three main approaches, i.e., redevelopment, wrapping, and migration. Redevelopment includes the rewriting from scratch approach and the reverse engineering approach. For reverse engineering of the legacy code, it often has to be understood first before rewriting it [12]. For representing the extracted information about the legacy source code and architecture a language independent meta-model like the KDM can be used [31]. The wrapping approach is divided into user interface wrapping, data wrapping, and function wrapping. In each wrapping approach the corresponding issue is wrapped so that the new system can access them. The migration approach is divided into component migration and system migration. In component migration, each component is migrated separately. In system migration, the whole legacy system is migrated at once.

There are different studies that researched which criteria lead to a software modernization decision [1, 38]. The three most relevant criteria are system usability, ending of technological support, and changes in business processes according to Koskinen et al. [38].

2.1.3 CloudMIG Approach

CloudMIG is a migration approach for software systems into the cloud developed by Frey et al. [15, 16, 17, 18, 19]. It comprises of six steps that are illustrated in Figure 2. These steps are described in the following.

A1 - Extraction

This step extracts architectural and utilization models of the legacy software system. The extraction utilizes KDM and Structured Metrics Meta-Model (SMM) as a language independent representation of a legacy software system and its quality attributes.

A2 - Selection

In the selection step an appropriate cloud profile candidate is chosen. Criteria for the decision can be a preference towards one cloud provider or a feature that has to be supported.

A3 - Generation

The output of the generation step is a generated target architecture and mapping model. In addition, the cloud environment constraint violations are detected in this step. A violation describes the breaking of a limitation of a specific cloud provider, for instance.

A4 - Adaptation

A reengineer might disagree with some aspects of the generated target architecture. Therefore, he can adjust them manually in this step.

A5 - Evaluation

The evaluation step simulates the performance and costs of the generated target architecture and evaluates it basing on the results.

A6 - Transformation

The actual transformation towards the generated target architecture. Currently, CloudMIG does not provide further support for performing this step. Thus, the source code and other artifacts have to be adopted manually.

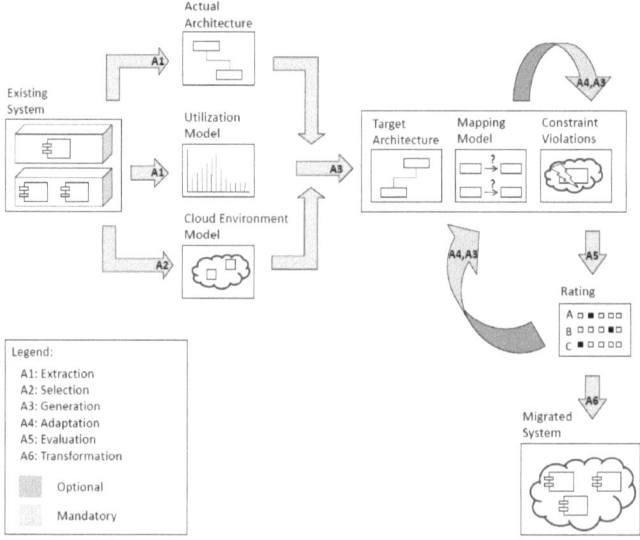

Figure 2: CloudMIG approach taken from Frey et al. [19]

```
1  <s₀ , (e₀ , t₀) , s₁ , (e₁ , t₁) , s₂ , (e₂ , t₂)  ... >
```

Listing 1: Evolution of a system

2.1.4 Simulation

A computer simulation is a program that attempts to emulate a particular system. One type of simulation is *discrete-event simulation* [57]. In *discrete-event simulation* the evolution of a system is viewed as a sequence of the form shown in Listing 1. A system starts in the state s_0. Then, the event e_0 occurs at the timestamp t_0 which results the system to be in the state s_1 and so on. The timestamps t_i, where i is larger than 0, have to be nonnegative numbers and the t_i's have to be nondecreasing. With such a sequence representing an evolution of a given system, we can conclude properties of the system, e.g., if it reaches a steady state. Thus, we can draw conclusions about the real system.

Entities

Entities are models of real world objects. In CloudSim (see Section 2.2.1), for example, a data center is an entity. The former mentioned state of the simulation model is the state of all entities' attributes. If an attribute changes due to the occurrence of an event, a new state is entered. Furthermore, an entity can provide methods for triggering the change of its attributes or to generate new events.

Events

While the simulation is active, external or internal events are produced and sent to the entities at a specific timestamp. If the timestamp lies in the future in respect to the actual simulation time, the event is scheduled until the simulation time reaches the specific timestamp. The scheduler maintains a queue of pending events. The events in the queue are processed successively. When the queue is empty, the simulation typically terminates, if it does not expect further external events. In CloudSim, for instance, the triggering for the creation of a virtual machine instance is an event.

Time

In a simulation, we typically use a model time for representing the real time. Using a model time has different advantages. It provides more control over time because we need not care about execution time of calculations. Furthermore, with this abstraction from the real world, we conduct simulations faster than in real time in most cases. A simulation can take 10 minutes in real time for simulating a real world system evolution for, e.g., 24 hours. The model time advances while processing the events from the event scheduler.

2.1.5 Model Transformation

Czarnecki and Helsen [13] state two different kinds of model transformation, i.e., model-to-code and model-to-model transformations. In model-to-code transformations the authors distinguish visitor-based approaches and template-based approaches. Visitor-based approaches provide a visitor mechanism that generates code. Template-based approaches use templates to generated code. The templates typically consist of target text with metacode to access information from the source model. The authors distinguish model-to-model transformations by six different kinds. These are direct-manipulation approaches, relational approaches, graph-transformation-based approaches, structure-driven approaches, hybrid approaches, and other model-to-model approaches. For further details of these approaches refer to Czarnecki and Helsen [13].

Mens and Van Gorp [44] mention important characteristics of a model transformation. These are the level of automation, complexity of the transformation, and preservation. The level of automation should be classified as manually, often manual intervention needed, or automated. Considering the complexity of the transformation, the classification can range from small to heavy-duty transformations which require other tools and techniques. A model transformation should define the preservation that it keeps. For example, refactoring preserves the behavior but alters the structure.

Query/View/Transformation (QVT) [23, 53] is a standard for model transformations established by the Object Management Group (OMG). It defines three related model transformation languages. These are Relations, Operational Mappings, and Core. The QVT specification integrates Object Constraint Language (OCL) 2.0 and is a hybrid of declarative and imperative. It requires Meta Object Facility (MOF) 2.0 models to operate on. Atlas Transformation Language (ATL) is a QVT-like transformation language and is described in Section 2.2.5.

2.2 Involved Technologies

The following sections provide an overview of the technologies that are relevant in the context of our work.

2.2.1 CloudSim

CloudSim is a cloud computing system and application simulator developed by Calheiros et al. [7, 9, 10]. It provides different novel features. The first feature is the support of modeling and simulating large cloud computing environments with a single computer. The second feature is a self-contained platform for modeling clouds, the service brokers, and different policies for allocation, for instance. CloudSim also provides support for network connection simulation between nodes as the third main feature. Finally, it offers a facility for simulation of a federated cloud environment.

CloudSim has been successfully used by other researchers for simulating task scheduling in the cloud or power aware cloud computing [4, 8, 36, 58, 60], for instance.

The architecture of CloudSim is illustrated in Figure 3. The basis is formed by the CloudSim core simulation engine. It is used by the network, cloud resources,

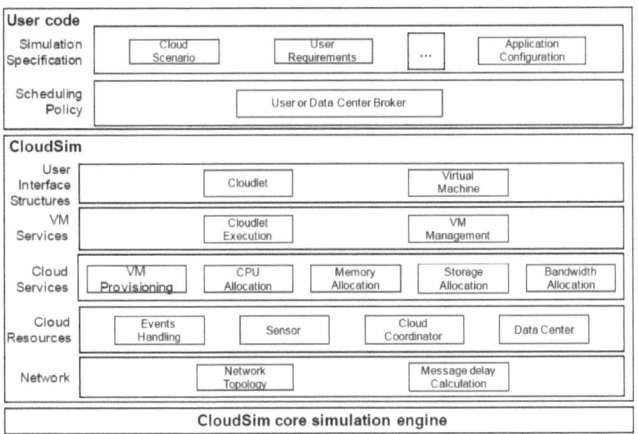

Figure 3: CloudSim architecture taken from Calheiros et al. [10]

cloud services, VM services and user interface structure. Here, so called Cloudlets constitute an important concept. CloudSim uses Cloudlets to simulate the application's execution by defining the total instruction count the application runtime would need. On the top, the user can specify the scheduling type (space-shared or time-shared) and other custom configurations.

CloudSim Meta-Model

We extracted the meta-model of CloudSim because there was no Ecore [65] model available. Figure 5 shows this meta-model as a Unified Modeling Language (UML) class diagram. The classes and associations left besides the class *link* mostly model the physical resources and the right side contains classes for modeling the virtual machines and Cloudlets. The *link* class provides a network link with a specific latency and bandwidth between *data centers* and *data center brokers*.

We start by describing the left part. A *data center* has storage and specific *data center characteristics* like the timezone or the virtual machine monitor. Furthermore, a *data center* has a *virtual machine allocation policy* that determines on which *host* a new *virtual machine* should be created. The *virtual machine allocation policy* and the *data center characteristics* share a list of available *hosts* that in the real world would be part of the *data center*. An important part of a *host* is a list of *processing elements (PE)*. A *PE* has a *PE provisioner* that provides the

13

MIPS, which is a measure for the computing performance. Furthermore, a *host* has a *bandwidth provisioner*, *RAM provisioner*, and *virtual machine scheduler*.

In the right part of Figure 5, the *data center broker* has a major role. It is responsible for the creation of *Cloudlets* and triggers the creation of *virtual machine* instances. Therefore, it maintains a list of created *Cloudlets* and *virtual machine* instances. A *virtual machine* instance has different attributes like MIPS and RAM. In addition, it is associated with a *Cloudlet scheduler* which is responsible for processing *Cloudlets*. The most important attribute of a *Cloudlet* is the *length*. In combination with the MIPS of a *virtual machine* instance, this attribute determines how long the *Cloudlet* is processing. In addition, a *Cloudlet* has other attributes and *utilization models* for RAM, CPU, and bandwidth.

In CloudSim, only *data centers* and *data center brokers* are simulation entities, i.e., all events can only be processed by those classes.

2.2.2 CloudMIG Xpress

CloudMIG Xpress [19] is a prototype implementation of the CloudMIG approach which was described in Section 2.1.3. It bases on the Eclipse Rich Client Platform. Figure 4 illustrates an overview of CloudMIG Xpress. It exhibits a plug-in based architecture and defines different interfaces for plug-ins that realize the steps A1, A3, and A5 of CloudMIG. CloudMIG's internal data format is the Cloud Environment Model (CEM). Currently, CloudMIG Xpress only supports the steps A1, A2, and partly A3. Our work contributes the step A5.

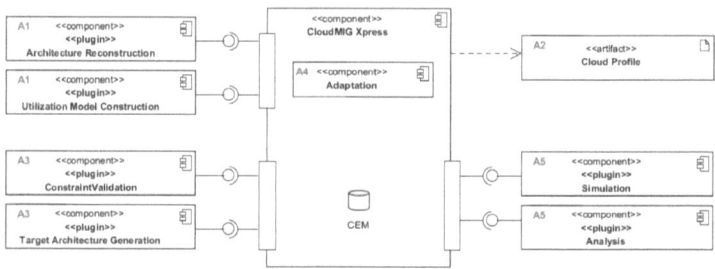

Figure 4: CloudMIG Xpress overview taken from Frey et al. [19]

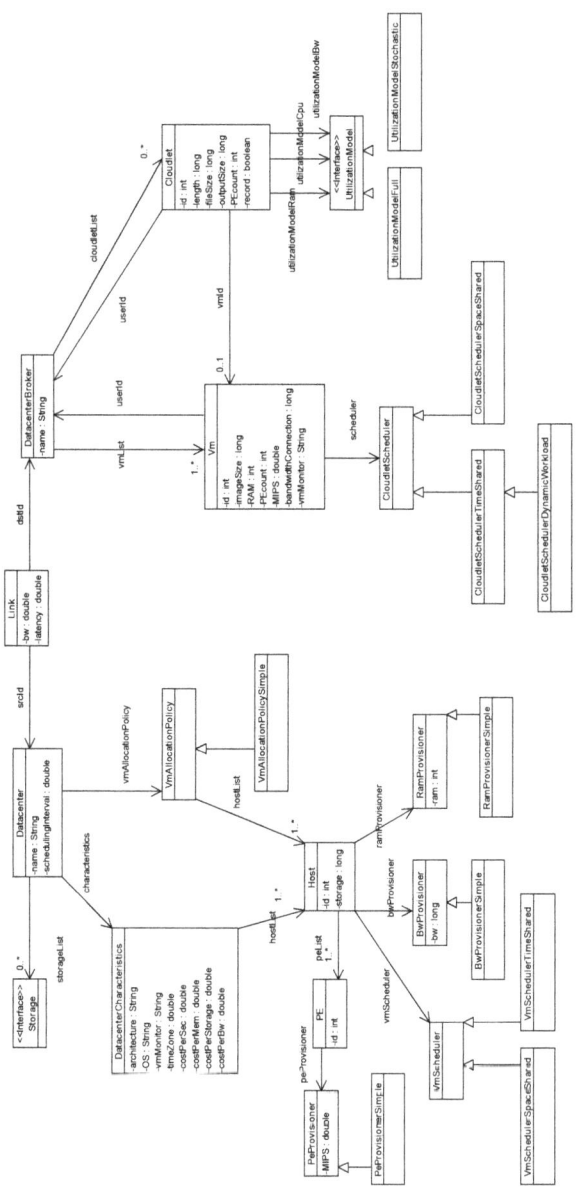

Figure 5: Extracted CloudSim meta-model

2.2.3 Knowledge Discovery Meta-Model

KDM [22] was created by the OMG and was defined as an ISO standard in 2011 [54]. KDM maps information about software assets, their associations, and operational environments into one common data interchange format. Then, different analysis tools have a common base for interchanging information. Thereby, the different architectural views, which can be extracted by various analysis tools, can be kept in one meta-model. For this purpose KDM provides various levels of abstraction represented by entities and relations. This section provides an overview of the structure and organization of KDM.

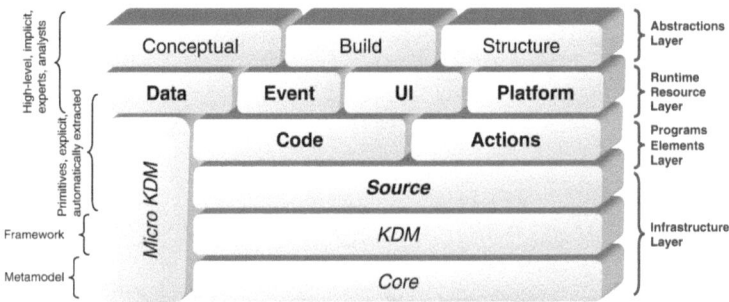

Figure 6: Layers of KDM taken from Pérez-Castillo et al. [54]

Figure 6 shows the four layers of KDM. These four layers are split into several packages. The remainder of the section describes the different layers and packages of KDM.

Infrastructure Layer

This layer describes the core components of KDM with the *core* and *kdm* packages. Every model in other layers inherits directly or indirectly from these components. The *source* package is also contained in this layer. It models the physical resources like source code files and images.

Program Layer

The program layer defines a language-independent representation of the existing source code with the *code* and *action* package. The former defines model elements for representing the logical structure, dependencies, classes, and methods. The latter models behavioral aspects of the software system by describing the control and data flow.

Resource Layer

Higher-level knowledge about the existing software system is represented in this layer. It contains the *data*, *event*, *UI*, and *platform* package. The *data* package handles persistent data aspects of an application. With the *event* package the different events that might occur can be modeled. The *UI* package contains elements to model aspects of the user interface. Last, the *platform* package provides means for modeling the artifacts that relate to the runtime platform.

Abstraction Layer

This layer contains the highest level of abstractions about the existing software system. The contained packages are the *conceptual*, *build*, and *structure* package. They represent knowledge about the conceptual perspective of the software system, the build system, and the higher level structure like a UML component diagram of the software system.

2.2.4 Structured Metrics Meta-Model

SMM [24] was developed in the context of the architecture-driven modernization (ADM) taskforce by the OMG. The specification defines an extensible meta-model for representing information regarding measurements relating to any structured model that is MOF-conform. Furthermore, SMM includes elements that can be used to express a wide range of software measures. Static and dynamic aspects of a software system can be modeled with the metrics in SMM. The SMM specification includes a minimal library of software measures for illustrative purposes.

2.2.5 Atlas Transformation Language

The Atlas Transformation Language (ATL) [33, 34] is a model-to-model transformation language. It is developed by the ATLAS INRIA and LINA research group. There exists also a tool called ATL IDE [35, 50] that is a toolkit on the basis of the Eclipse Modeling Framework (EMF). ATL can be used declaratively and imperatively, and is a QVT similar language. The preferred style of transformation

```
1  rule Attribute2Column {
2    from attr : UML!Attribute
3    to
4      col : DB!Column (
5        name <- attr.name
6      )
7  }
```

Listing 2: ATL declarative example taken from Bézivin et al. [5]

```
1  «IMPORT classdefinition»
2  «DEFINE javamain FOR Model»
3
4  «FILE "benchmarks/java/" + this.class.name + ".java"»
5    public class «this.class.name» {
6      public static void main(String[] args) {
7        System.out.println("Hello World");
8      }
9    }
10 «ENDFILE»
11 «ENDDEFINE»
```

Listing 3: Xpand hello world template for Java

is writing in the declarative way. However, for transformations that are hard to express in a declarative way, it also provides the imperative style.

An ATL transformation is composed of rules. These rules define on which elements they are executed and what elements are created from the input.

Listing 2 shows a declarative example of ATL. The example rule takes a UML attribute in line 2 and transforms this attribute into a column of a database in line 4 by naming the column with the attribute name in line 5.

2.2.6 Xpand

Xpand [66] is a statically-typed template language which is available as an Eclipse plug-in. It is specialized on code generation based on EMF models. Xpand requires a meta-model, an instance of this meta-model, a template, and a workflow for the generation. The Xpand language is a domain-specific language (DSL) that has a small but sufficient vocabulary like `FOR` and `FOREACH` for applying templates. An integrated editor provides syntax coloring, error highlighting, and code completion. Xpand was originally developed as part of the openArchitectureWare [51] project.

Listing 3 shows an example template for the generation of a *Hello World* program in Java. Line 1 imports the — omitted for shortness — meta-model *classdefinition* which contains a class *Model* which has an attribute *class* of type *Class*. The *Class* class has an attribute *name*. In line 2, a template for the type *Model* is started. Afterwards, line 4 expresses that the output of the enclosing FILE tag should be written to a file named benchmarks/java/*class.name*.java. Line 5 to 9 define a Java class with the name *class.name* and a main method that prints Hello World on the console. Line 10 closes the FILE tag and line 11 closes the started template for the type Model.

3 Simulation Input

This section describes the input for simulation of a cloud deployment option with CloudSim including our conducted enhancements. Section 3.1 provides an overview of the required input parameters. Afterwards, Sections 3.2 to 3.9 describe the required input parameters and the approaches for deriving them.

3.1 Overview

The input parameters MIPIPS and instruction count are related to *instructions*. The MIPIPS serve as a measure for the performance of a CPU. They are described in Section 3.2. The instruction count of a method serves as an indicator for the work that has to be conducted by the CPU if the method is called. Section 3.3 describes three different approaches for the derivation of the instruction count of a method.

Instructions in general can be instructions on a low level machine language like Assembler, on an intermediate level like Java bytecode, or on the level of a high level language like Java. For this thesis, we define instructions as a well defined set of statements that lies between the intermediate level and the high level language definition. As instructions we define declarations of a variable, assignments with at least one operation on the right hand side like x = 3 + 2, comparisons, field accesses, and class creations.

Most of the time when we talk about instructions, we mean integer plus instructions. We define an integer plus instruction as the assignment to a variable and on the right hand side of the assignment two integer types are combined with a plus statement, e.g., x = y + 3 where y is an integer variable. For simplicity and shortness, we omit integer plus and simply write instructions, if the meaning is unambiguous.

Section 3.4 describes weights that are used to convert, for instance, a double minus instruction to integer plus instructions. In Section 3.5 the size of a data type or class in bytes is derived. This is needed for the simulation of network traffic. Section 3.6 describes the input of an SMM workload profile which is required for creating the Cloudlets. In Section 3.7 the enriched KDM model is described. Then, Section 3.8 presents the adaptation rules which are used for starting and terminating virtual machine instances during runtime. Finally, Section 3.9 describes the simulation configuration parameters.

3.2 MIPIPS

This section describes what mega integer plus instructions per second (MIPIPS) are and why we need them. Furthermore, our benchmark for derivation of MIPIPS is explained in Section 3.2.2.

3.2.1 Description

CloudSim requires MIPS as a measure for the computing performance of virtual machine instances. However, we consider MIPS as too coarse grained. Most CPUs need different times for different low level instructions. For example, a division of two doubles typically takes longer than an addition of two integers on current CPUs. Furthermore, CloudSim does not suggest how to measure MIPS.

We introduce MIPIPS as the measure for describing the computing performance and express instructions like double plus as integer plus instructions through a conversion. Notably, we could have used, e.g., mega double plus instructions per second (MDPIPS) as the measure for computing performance and normalized all other instructions to double plus instructions (see Section 3.4 for details). However, we wanted an underlying instruction type that is faster than most other instructions because the conversion factors become more readable. For example, if we would have used a class creation instruction, mostly all other instructions would be between 0 and 1, and saying that one integer plus can be performed in 0.0004 class creation instructions is improper.

We do not use already existing benchmarks like Dhrystone (see Section 9.7) or Cloudstone (see Section 9.8) because we need an easily adaptable to new programming languages benchmark and we later describe an approach for counting instructions that bases on static analysis which needs an association between statements and the measure for computing performance.

Our MIPIPS benchmark measures the computing performance of a single core. Hence, a computer with one core will have the same MIPIPS value as a computer with 64 cores, if the performance of the one core on the first computer equals the performance of one core on the second computer. This is motivated by the fact that a program which is single-threaded is not faster on a computer with 64 cores. Furthermore, if the program has, e.g., two threads for processing, the performance depends on the synchronization method used in the program. However, the core count is also considered in the simulation. CloudSim defines the value *TotalMIPS* which is calculated by multiplying the core count with the MIPS. In accordance to this definition, we define *TotalMIPIPS* as the product of the core count and the MIPIPS value.

3.2.2 Derivation

The basic idea for deriving MIPIPS is a benchmark that measures the runtime of a defined amount of integer plus instructions.

The runtime of a single instruction cannot be measured accurately because measurement techniques like the usage of `System.currentTimeMillis()` in Java have a resolution of one millisecond. Even CPU cycle counters are not sufficient accurate. Hence, we use a loop which runs our integer plus instructions at least for ten seconds on current CPUs. Measuring the runtime of the whole loop would include more instructions like jumps and comparisons being measured. Therefore, we do a calibration run (see Listing 4) for running the loop and then do a second run with our integer plus instructions added to the loop's body (see Listing 5). Afterwards, we subtract the runtime of the second run from the first run. This reveals the execution time of the added integer plus instructions.

Our runtime measuring technique is a program that acts as master and starts the benchmark run in a slave on the same machine. The runtime measurement is conducted by the slave program due to exclusion of initialization time. After the execution, the slave returns the measured runtime for the benchmark run to the master. According to Georges et al. [20], this measurement must be done at least 30 times. Hence optimally, the master starts the slave 30 times for each benchmark. The number of runs can be configured by parameters or from a GUI (see Section 6 for details). Afterwards, the master calculates the median of the response times.

An important part is the disablement of optimizations for the compiler and interpreter when the slave program is called by the master program. Depending on the selected language and optimization settings, the optimization can cause our loop to have constant runtime.

Listing 4 shows the calibration run in Java. Line 1 declares an integer variable named x that is incremented by 2 in the loop body at line 7. The variable x is incremented by 2 because an increment of 1 can be optimized in many languages. This integer variable is printed to the console in line 14. The purpose of this variable and printing of it is that the compiler cannot easily omit the loop. Line 3, and 11 to 13 show the applied runtime measurement of the loop. In line 6 to 9 the actual loop

```
1  int x = 0;
2
3  long startTime = System.currentTimeMillis();
4
5  int i = -2147483647;
6  while (i < 2147483647) {
7    x = x + 2;
8    i += 1;
9  }
10
11 long endTime = System.currentTimeMillis();
12 long difftime = endTime - startTime;
13 System.out.println(difftime);
14 System.out.println(x);
```

Listing 4: Calibration for running the loop without added integer plus instructions in Java

is displayed. Notably, this is a direct translation from a for loop to a while loop. Our first approach contained a for loop. However, at least the Microsoft C# compiler in version 4.0.30319.1 optimizes for loops, though we disabled optimization. With this compiler, a while loop is not optimized when optimization is disabled.

Listing 5 shows the MIPIPS counter. Compared to the calibration, line 2, 9, and 17 are added. These lines declare a variable y, add 3 to y in the while loop, and finally print the value of y. y is incremented by 3 because otherwise the compiler can use the value of x and does not need to calculate y.

For the derivation of the added instruction count of the benchmark, the benchmark reads in the instruction count from a comment at the top of the class. Subsequently, the instruction count is divided by the median of the runtime in seconds. This value is the derived MIPIPS for the platform. Notably, the derivation needs to be rerun whenever a new software is installed that should act as a permanent service on the machine because the runtime of the benchmark can be larger due to the changed workload on the CPU.

Benchmark Generation with Xpand

For supporting easy adaptability for new programming languages, we utilize Xpand to generate the benchmark for different target languages. Xpand requires a meta-model definition, an instance of the meta-model, and a language-specific generation template.

```
 1  int x = 0;
 2  int y = 0;
 3
 4  long startTime = System.currentTimeMillis();
 5
 6  int i = -2147483647;
 7  while (i < 2147483647) {
 8      x = x + 2;
 9      y = y + 3;
10      i += 1;
11  }
12
13  long endTime = System.currentTimeMillis();
14  long difftime = endTime - startTime;
15  System.out.println(difftime);
16  System.out.println(x);
17  System.out.println(y);
```

Listing 5: MIPIPS counter in Java

The meta-model, following the Ecore definition, for representation of a benchmark class is shown in Appendix B. It contains the basic elements of an imperative programing language. It enables the modeling of classes, methods, expressions, variable declarations, loops, class creations, and concrete method calls. Furthermore, it contains a class for an empty line, which supports the readability of the generated output. Two special classes are included in the meta-model. These are *SystemOut* which represents the statement for printing Strings to the console and *MeasureTime* which represents the statement for getting the current value of a time counter. These two classes are mapped by the generation template to individual statements for each target language and can be quite different like `System.out.println()` for Java and `puts` for Ruby.

Listing 6 shows the MIPIPS counter in the language independent XML representation which is an instance of the class definition meta-model. A generated code example for Java was already presented in Listing 5 and described before. Hence, we only describe the special facts about this example in XML representation. The class definition contains a *instructionCount* attribute in line 5. This attribute is included in the concrete language representation as a comment at the beginning of the class and only required by the master program. From this comment the master program gets the information about the instruction count of the benchmark which

```xml
<?xml version="1.0" encoding="ASCII"?>
<classdefinition:Model xmi:version="2.0"
  xmlns:xmi="http://www.omg.org/XMI" xmlns:xsi="http://www.w3.org/2001/XMLSchema-instance"
  xmlns:classdefinition="http://www.example.org/classdefinition" xsi:schemaLocation="http://www.example.org/classdefinition ../metamodel/classdefinition.ecore">
  <class name="MIPIPSCounter" namespace="benchmarks" instructionCount="4294967295">
    <methods exporttype="public" modifier="static" returntype="void" name="main">
      <parameters name="args" type="String[]"/>
      <statements xsi:type="classdefinition:VariableDeclaration" variablename="x" initializer="0">
        <type xsi:type="classdefinition:Datatype" name="int"/>
      </statements>
      <statements xsi:type="classdefinition:VariableDeclaration" variablename="y" initializer="0">
        <type xsi:type="classdefinition:Datatype" name="int"/>
      </statements>
      <statements xsi:type="classdefinition:EmptyLine"/>
      <statements xsi:type="classdefinition:MeasureTime" type="long" variablename="startTime"/>
      <statements xsi:type="classdefinition:EmptyLine"/>
      <statements xsi:type="classdefinition:ForLoop" variabletype="int" variablename="i" initializer="-2147483647" conditionCheck="&lt;" conditionValue="2147483647" stepFunction="+=1">
        <statements xsi:type="classdefinition:Expression" leftSide="x" rightSide="x + 2"/>
        <statements xsi:type="classdefinition:Expression" leftSide="y" rightSide="y + 3"/>
      </statements>
      <statements xsi:type="classdefinition:EmptyLine"/>
      <statements xsi:type="classdefinition:MeasureTime" type="long" variablename="endTime"/>
      <statements xsi:type="classdefinition:VariableDeclaration" variablename="difftime" initializer="endTime - startTime">
        <type xsi:type="classdefinition:Datatype" name="long"/>
      </statements>
      <statements xsi:type="classdefinition:SystemOut" text="difftime"/>
      <statements xsi:type="classdefinition:SystemOut" text="x"/>
      <statements xsi:type="classdefinition:SystemOut" text="y"/>
    </methods>
  </class>
</classdefinition:Model>
```

Listing 6: MIPIPS counter in language independent XML representation is used for the MIPIPS calculation. The instruction count is derived by calculating the iteration count and taking this as the instruction count because only one instruction is added and this instruction is executed only once in every loop iteration.

If a new language shall be supported by the whole benchmark, the programmer simply has to add a generation template for the desired language. He does not need to change the declarations of each benchmark. Currently, we support the languages Java, C, C++, C#, Python, and Ruby.

3.3 Instruction Count

Section 3.3.1 describes our approaches for deriving the instruction count from an application which is represented as a KDM instance. Then, Section 3.3.2 provides an overview of the different approaches for derivation. In Sections 3.3.3 to 3.3.5 the approaches are described.

3.3.1 Description

The instruction count is needed as a representation of the work that must be conducted for a call to a program or web service. In combination with the MIPIPS, the instruction count approximates the runtime on the computer that has the corresponding MIPIPS. For example, assume 2 MIPIPS and 100,000 instructions for a call to a web service. Then, the runtime of the call to the web service will be approximately 50 milliseconds.

3.3.2 Derivation Overview

We consider different possible preconditions for the derivation on which a specific approach can be chosen. The first approach, named *dynamic approach*, requires an instance of the code package of KDM, results of a dynamic analysis with contained response times, and the MIPIPS of the computer where the dynamic analysis took place. It is described in Section 3.3.3 and utilizes the method definitions in the KDM instance and response times from the dynamic analysis. The second approach, named *static approach*, requires instances of the code and action package of KDM. The action package contains statements like variable declarations and condition blocks. The contained statements are counted in the *static approach* (see Section 3.3.4). Both approaches have shortcomings which we address and describe in our third approach, named *hybrid approach*, in Section 3.3.5, which has the preconditions of the *dynamic approach* and *static approach*. Table 1 shows an overview for the preconditions for each approach.

Approach	Preconditions
dynamic approach	1. Instance of the code package of KDM
	2. Response times from a dynamic analysis
	3. MIPIPS of the node of the dynamic analysis
static approach	1. Instance of the code and action package of KDM
hybrid approach	1. Instance of the code and action package of KDM
	2. Response times from a dynamic analysis
	3. MIPIPS of the node of the dynamic analysis

Table 1: Overview of the preconditions for each instruction count derivation approach

3.3.3 Dynamic Approach

One precondition of the *dynamic approach* is the availability of response times from a dynamic analysis. This means, that response times have to be monitored at runtime of the software under study. Optimally, there exists a phase of only low CPU utilization in the dynamic analysis such that the response times result from the execution of the method's instructions without major scheduling effects. Furthermore, the MIPIPS of the computer, where the dynamic analysis took place, have to be available. First, the *dynamic approach* computes the median response times for each method in the workload. The method for determining the median of response times during phases of low CPU utilization is described in the following section. The instruction count of each method in millions is calculated by multiplying the median response time with the MIPIPS of the platform that measured the response time. For example, the median of response time is 20 milliseconds and the MIPIPS is 200. The resulting instruction count in millions is $0.020 \cdot 200 = 4$.

Notably, often not all methods are contained in the monitored workload. These methods get a -1 instruction count which indicates that those methods have no instruction count and that an error must be thrown when they are accessed in the simulation.

Determining the Median of Response Times during phases of Low CPU Utilization

The *dynamic approach* requires the median of response times that result from the execution of the methods. Typically, the response time depends on many factors like disk writing latency and other method executions that have a higher priority in a time-shared scheduler. A high influence factor is the availability of CPU time, i.e., whether the method can directly be processed and does not need to wait for execution. Figure 7 shows the response times of an example run with two peeks in hour 7 and 17. Most likely, the two peeks in Figure 7 are caused by the high CPU utilization at the corresponding time. However, our simulation should simulate these peeks by simulating the CPU utilization. Hence, we need the response time that the method has during phases of low CPU utilization.

In Figure 7, the set of response times that best suits our needs is marked by a red rectangle. Notably, there are lower response times. Hence, the response time we seek is not the minimum of the response times. Our approach is to find the group of smallest response times with n elements. Therefore, we traverse the response times minute for minute and insert each found response time in its corresponding group. A group is formed by its basic value plus and minus a threshold of 1 millisecond. The basic value is the first value that is inserted into the group. For example, the first value in Figure 7 is about 47 milliseconds. This value opens a new group that has the basic value 47 milliseconds. All new response times that lie between 46 and 48 milliseconds are inserted in this group. If a group reaches n group elements, the group is treated as a candidate for the response times during phases of low CPU utilization. Now, only response times that are smaller than this group must be inserted into new groups. If there are no further response times available, the algorithm terminates and returns the median of the candidate group. If no candidate group was found, the algorithm returns the median value of the group that has the smallest response times values. We set n to 30 in our tool. This value performed best in our tests.

3.3.4 Static Approach

The *static approach* requires KDM instances that contain the code and action package of the software under analysis. It iterates over all methods and counts the instructions in an accumulator variable for each method. Then, the instruction count is annotated to each method. In the following, we describe the counting method

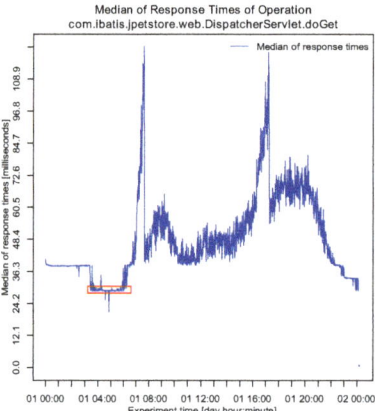

Figure 7: Example of determining the median of response times during phases of low CPU utilization in the dynamic approach

for the most used control flow statements in programming languages, i.e., condition blocks, loops, try-catch-finally, and calls. For simplicity and easier understanding, every statement in these sections is counted with a weight of 1. The last section abolishes this restriction.

Condition Blocks

The instruction count for each path i (ic_{path_i}) of n paths in the condition block is calculated. Here, we define a path as the condition body of the branch, for instance in if (x > 0) then y = 0 the y = 0 is the path. The instructions are counted in the condition clause (ic_{clause_i}) and the other condition clauses' instructions, that were calculated before, are added. This instruction count is then added to the instruction count of the path with was multiplied before with the probability of the path ($prob_{path_i}$). The final result of the instruction count for the condition block is the sum of those factors. The resulting calculation formula for derivation of the instruction count of a condition block ($ic_{condition\_block}$) is displayed in Equation 1.

$$(1) \qquad ic_{condition\_block} = \sum_{i=0}^{n-1} (\sum_{j=0}^{i} ic_{clause_j}) + ic_{path_i} \cdot prob_{path_i}$$

```
1  if (i == 5) {
2      i = 3;
3      x = 5;
4      y = x + i;
5  } else if (i == 6) {
6      i = 9;
7  } else {
8      i = 10;
9  }
```

Listing 7: Example of deriving the instruction count from a condition block

Without a data flow analysis, it is hard to predict how often a specific path in a condition block will be taken. This motivates the basic assumption that every path of the condition block is taken with a specific probability of 1 divided by the number of paths n of the condition block. A missing else statement is interpreted as an empty path. Hence, an *if* statement without an *else* has the probability of $\frac{1}{2}$. With means of a data flow analysis, the probability can, of course, be further refined. However, we did not implement data flow analysis due to a lack of time.

Listing 7 shows an example. The instruction count for each path is calculated. The first condition body has three instructions (line 2 to 4), the second condition body has one instruction (line 6), and the last condition body has one instruction (line 8). The first condition clause has one instruction (line 1), the second condition clause has one instruction (line 5) plus the one instruction for the first condition clause (line 1), and the last condition clause has no instructions (line 7) plus two instructions of the prior condition clauses. The probability of each path is assumed to be $\frac{1}{3}$. The resulting instruction count for the condition block is $(1 + 3 \cdot \frac{1}{3}) + ((1 + 1) + 1 \cdot \frac{1}{3}) + ((1 + 1 + 0) + 1 \cdot \frac{1}{3}) = 6\frac{2}{3}$.

Appendix C shows the KDM representation of the class *IfClass* which is displayed in Listing 8 in Java. The *ClassUnit* in line 6 represents the *IfClass*. In line 11 the *main* method is defined. Lines 32 to 42 represent the `int i = 5` statement. The condition block ranges from line 44 to line 81. The condition clause is shown in the lines 48 to 60. The condition body is displayed in the lines 61 to 80. For instruction counting, it is first searched for an *if* statement which begins in line 44. Then, the instructions in the condition clause are counted. The algorithm finds the *EQUALS* element which is one instruction. Hence, the condition clause has one instruction. Then, the instructions in the condition body are counted. The *ASSIGN* element

```
 1  package examplepackage;
 2
 3  public class IfClass {
 4    public static void main(String[] args) {
 5      int i = 5;
 6      if (i == 5) {
 7        i = 3;
 8      }
 9    }
10  }
```

Listing 8: Example class for deriving the instruction count from a condition block from a KDM instance

represents one instruction. An *else if* statement is not found and hence there are two paths. Thus, the instruction count for the condition block sums up to $1 + 1 \cdot \frac{1}{2} = 1 \frac{1}{2}$.

For Loops

In *for* loops with a static analyzable bound, the iterating count ($iter_{count}$) can be derived by the absolute value of the bound minus the initial value and then divided by the absolute value of the changing step of the iterating variable in each loop, which is 1 in `i++`, for example. In most *for* loops, there is an initialization of the iterating variable that exhibits an own instruction count (ic_{init}), an end condition with an instruction count ($ic_{cond_{end}}$), and a change of the iterating variable with an instruction count ($ic_{iter_{change}}$). The sum of the later values is added to the instruction count of the loop (ic_{loop}). Then, the sum is multiplied with the iteration count. Finally, the instruction count of the initialization is added to the resulting value. The formula for calculation of a *for* statement (ic_{for_loop}). is displayed in Equation 2.

If there is no static analyzable bound like in *for each* loops, for instance, it cannot simply be determined how often the loop will be executed. In this case, we assume a configurable constant value which is provided by the user for the iteration count. The same is done for *while* and *do while* loops, if there is no direct translation to a *for* loop.

Break, continue, return, goto statements, and explicit changing of the iteration variable can influence the iteration count. In order to support those statements in instruction count derivation, there has to be some data flow analysis. We did not implement data flow analysis due to lack of time and thus, break and continue statements are simply ignored.

```
1  for (int i = 0; i < 10; i++) {
2      x = i + 3;
3  }
```

Listing 9: Example of deriving the instruction count from a *for* loop

(2) $$ic_{for\_loop} = ic_{init} + (iter_{count} \cdot (ic_{cond_{end}} + ic_{iter_{change}} + ic_{loop}))$$

Listing 9 displays an example for a simple *for* loop instruction count derivation. The initialization of the iterating variable i takes 1 instruction. The iteration count is calculated by $|(10-0)|/|1|$ and hence it is 10. The body of the loop has 1 instruction (line 2). The step change in each iteration takes 1 instruction and the condition also takes 1 instruction (line 1). This results in $1 + (10 \cdot (1 + 1 + 1)) = 31$ instructions.

Try-catch-finally Statements

Our approach assumes that catch statements are used for unexpected exceptions that might happen. The try block with its instruction count (ic_{try}) is called every time the *try-catch-finally* statement is executed. However, the catch block with the instruction count (ic_{catch_i}) for each catch statement i of n catch statements is only executed, if an error occurs which happens with a specific probability ($prob_{catch_i}$). The occurrence of an error is assumed to be independent from the occurrence of other errors. The probability of an unexpected exception highly depends on, for example, the runtime environment. In an environment with rather unreliable wireless connection a network exception can be thrown many times, for instance. We assume that errors only occur in one percent of the cases. This number is motivated by assuming a normal distribution with $\alpha = 0.01$ for an occurrence of an error. The finally block with its instruction count ($ic_{finally}$) is by definition called every time the *try-catch-finally* statement is executed. Equation 3 shows the resulting formula for calculation of a *try-catch-finally* statement ($ic_{try-catch-finally}$).

(3) $$ic_{try-catch-finally} = ic_{try} + (\sum_{i=0}^{n-1} prob_{catch_i} \cdot ic_{catch_i}) + ic_{finally}$$

```
 1  try {
 2      stream.open();
 3      stream.write();
 4  } catch (IOException e) {
 5      e.printStackTrace();
 6  } catch (FileNotFoundException e) {
 7      e.printStackTrace();
 8      x = 3;
 9  } finally {
10      stream.close();
11      x = 0;
12  }
```

Listing 10: Example of deriving the instruction count from a *try-catch-finally* statement

Listing 10 displays an example for deriving the instruction count from a *try-catch-finally* statement. The try block in line 1 to 3 has 2 instructions. The first catch block in line 4 and 5 has 1 instruction and probability 0.01, and the second catch block in 6 to 8 takes 2 instructions and probability 0.01. The final block in line 9 to 11 has 2 instructions. The instruction count for the *try-catch-finally*-statement is then $2 + (0.01 \cdot 1 + 0.01 \cdot 2) + 2 = 4.03$.

Calls

The instructions of a method call are counted with the annotated instruction count plus the instructions of the concrete parameters, if the method was already counted. If this annotation does not exist, the instructions in the called method (ic_{called_method}) are counted at first. This approach may lead to a cycle which would result in an endless loop. Hence, we mark a method that is currently counted and check before counting, whether it is already counting. If this mark exists, we detected a cyclic dependency and approximate the called method by a constant number of instructions which is provided by the user. Notably, a method implementing recursion contains a cycle. Instruction counts of the concrete parameters must be also considered. For each parameter the instruction count ($ic_{parameter_i}$) must be derived because the parameter might be a statement like x + 4 or even a call to another method. The formula for deriving the instruction count for method calls (ic_{method_call}) is shown in Equation 4. A special method call is the creation of a new object which has its own deriving method for its instruction ($ic_{object\_creation}$) (see Equation 5). The instruction counting for the creation of an object is the counting of the constructor

```java
public void method1() {
    x = method2(3, "example", method3());
}

public int method2(int i, String x, long y) {
    System.out.println(x);
    return i-1;
}

public long method3() {
    return 3;
}
```

Listing 11: Example of deriving the instruction count from a method call

call ($ic_{constructor_{own}}$) and its parameters ($ic_{parameter_i}$) and the initialization of declared attributes ($ic_{attributes_{own}}$). Notably, the instruction count of the constructor includes the instruction count of its possible parent constructor.

Method calls to, e.g., libraries can only be counted if the source code is available. Otherwise the instruction count of those methods is a constant configurable by the user.

$$ic_{method\_call} = ic_{called\_method} + \sum_{i=0}^{n-1} ic_{parameter_i} \tag{4}$$

$$ic_{object\_creation} = ic_{attributes} + ic_{constructor} + \sum_{i=0}^{n-1} ic_{parameter_i} \tag{5}$$

Listing 11 displays an example for deriving the instruction count from a method calls' statements. It starts with counting the instructions of *method1* which results in 1 instruction for the assignment plus the instructions of the method call to *method2* in line 2. *method2* has 1 instruction for line 7 plus the call to `System.out.println` in line 6, which is unknown and assumed with a constant instruction count provided by the user. We assume here 100 instructions as an example. Thus, the instruction count of *method2* is 101. The parameters of the method call to *method2* have the instruction count $1 + 1 + 1 = 3$ which results from the fact that *method3* has 1 instruction. The instruction count of the call to *method2* in *method1* totals up to $101 + 3 = 104$.

```
1  new Class2(2 + 3);
2
3  class Class2 {
4    private int attrib1 = 0;
5    private int attrib2 = 3;
6
7    public Class2(int x) {
8      attrib1 = x;
9    }
10 }
```

Listing 12: Example of deriving the instruction count from a new object creation

```
1  int x1 = 0;
2  int x2 = 3;
3  int x3 = x1 - x2;
4  int x3 = x1 / x2;
5
6  long y1 = 4000;
7  long y2 = 1000;
8  long y3 = y1 + y2;
9  long y4 = y1 * y2;
```

Listing 13: Example of deriving the instruction count with weights

Listing 12 displays an example for deriving the instruction count from a new object creation. In line 1 a new object of *Class2* is created. The instruction count for this class creation is the instruction count of the constructor body which is 1 (line 8) plus the initializations of the attributes (line 4 and 5) which take in sum 2 instructions. The parameter to the constructor has 1 instruction. Thus, the instruction count is $1 + 2 + 1 = 5$.

Weight per Specific Statement

In most environments adding two, for example, double values will consume more time than adding two integer values. In general, a plus in the code on different data types can have a significant difference in the performance. For satisfaction of this issue, we propose a special weight per specific statement. With this weight, a plus instruction can count four integer plus instructions for double values instead of only one integer plus instruction, for instance. The derivation of the weights for each platform is discussed in Section 3.4.

Data type	Statement	Weight
int	-	2
int	/	3
long	+	4
long	*	8

Table 2: Example weights

Listing 13 shows an example for instruction counting with different weights. The weights for the example are listed in Table 2. Line 1 and 2 declare two integer variables. In line 3 the *static approach* searches for an integer minus statement in the weight table and finds the weight 2 which is the instruction count for the expression in line 3. For line 4 it searches for an integer divide statement in the weight table and finds the weight 3. Line 6 and 7 declare two long variables. Again, the *static approach* searches for the expression in line 8 in the weight table but now for a long plus statement and finds 4. The resulting instruction count of line 8 is thus 4 instructions. For line 9 the *static approach* searches for a long multiply statement and finds the weight 8 which is the resulting instruction count.

3.3.5 Hybrid Approach

This approach combines the advantages of the *dynamic approach* and *static approach* and thus rules out some disadvantages of the former ones. The *dynamic approach* considers the real runtime of a method and thus can predict the runtime of a method very closely. However, it cannot derive an instruction count for every method because data from dynamic analysis is often incomplete. The *static approach* often results in wrong instruction counts because it does not consider optimization from the compiler, for instance. However, it can derive an instruction count for every method.

To combine the advantages, we take the instruction counts from the *dynamic approach* and try to correct the instruction counts from the *static approach*. Furthermore, the missing values for the instruction count of methods in the *dynamic approach* are filled with the instruction count from the *static approach*.

Determining the Probability of a Path for a Condition Block

The *static approach* assumes even distribution for all paths in a condition block. However, in most cases this assumption proves wrong. With the instruction counts from the *dynamic approach*, we can calculate a better approximation for the prob-

```
1  if (x == 0) then
2     method1();
3  else if (x == 1) then
4     method2();
5  else
6     method3();
```

Listing 14: Example of determining the probability of a path for a condition block

abilities (p_i) of each path. The probability is important when we want to explicitly model separate submethods for the derivation of how often the submethod is called. The probability is calculated with the support of the instruction count (ic_{target}) for the whole condition block and the instruction counts for each path (ic_{path_i}) from the *static approach*. The two formulas are shown in Equation 6 and Equation 7 for n paths. The first equation reflects the condition that the instruction count of the condition block is the sum of instruction count for each path multiplied with its probability. The second equation describes the condition that probabilities sum up to 1 which results from the mathematical probability axioms. Notably, there is in general no unique solution for the variables p_i, if n is larger than 2. Therefore, we defined an auxiliary condition which is shown in Equation 8. This condition states that one probability p_i with a fixed i is larger than the other probabilities and the other probabilities must be equal to each other. Hence, only one probability is incremented at a time and all other probabilities decrement by the same decrement step. We defined this condition because it was the simplest condition in respect to programming effort and finding a unique solution for each probability.

$$(6) \qquad ic_{target} = \sum_{i=0}^{n-1} p_i \cdot ic_{path_i}$$

$$(7) \qquad 1 = \sum_{i=0}^{n-1} p_i$$

$$(8) \qquad \text{Let } i \in [0..n-1]: \quad p_1 = ... = p_j = ... = p_{n-1} <= p_i \ (j \neq i)$$

In Listing 14 an example application of the approach is shown. We assume that the path with *method1* has 5 instructions, the path with *method2* has 10 instructions, and the path with *method3* has 15 instructions. The instruction count determined by the *dynamic approach* for the condition block is assumed with 12 instructions. We start with $\frac{1}{3}$ as probability for each path which reveals 10 instructions for the conditional block. We add 0.01 to the first path and subtract 0.005 from the second and third path. The resulting instruction count for this combination is 9.925. Since the instruction count is lower than the instruction count for even distribution which was 10, the approach passes to the second path for factor change. The probabilities are reset to $\frac{1}{3}$. The changing of the second probability also results in 9.925 instructions and hence the approach passes to the third path for changing the probabilities. The probabilities are reset to $\frac{1}{3}$. The probability of the first and the second path is now 0.328333 and for the third path it is 0.343333 which results in 10.074 instructions. This is repeated until the approach finishes with probability of 0.2 for the first and second path, and 0.6 for the third path.

Correcting Wrong Instruction Count of Static Approach

The *static approach* mostly overestimates the instruction count because compiler and runtime optimization techniques like JIT can reduce the required instruction count. If a method has an instruction count assigned by the *dynamic approach*, the instruction count represents the possibly optimized method. If this method surely calls another method, which its instruction count resulted from the *static approach*, the instruction count of the called method cannot be higher than the instruction count of the caller. Hence, we set the instruction count of the called method to the instruction count of the caller method. If the caller method contains further statements, those statements are counted first and then subtracted from the instruction count that the called method is assigned.

Listing 15 shows an example where the *static approach* performs bad in practice. We assume that *method1* and *method2* are called at the top level and hence their instruction count is derived with the *dynamic approach*. It attributes 50 instructions to *method1* and 100 instructions to *method2*. The instruction count of *method3* can only be derived by the *static approach*. The *static approach* counts 3001 instructions for *method3*. Now all methods are searched for method calls that are conducted without being nested in a condition, i.e., where the probability of a call is 1.0. *Method1* calls *method3*. However, it calls *method3* with a probability of about 0.016 which is calculated by the former described approach for determining the probability

```
public void method1() {
  if (x == 0) then
    method3();
}

public void method2() {
  method3();
}

public void method3() {
  for (int i = 0; i < 1000; i++) {
    x = i + 3;
  }
}
```

Listing 15: Example of correcting a wrong instruction count of the static approach

of a condition block. *Method2* also calls *method3*. This time the calling probability is 1.0. Hence, *method3* can not take more time than *method2* and thus *method3*'s instruction count is set to 100 which is the instruction count of *method2*.

3.4 Weights per Statement

This section describes how the weights for each statement are derived.

3.4.1 Description

The *static approach* requires weights for different statements such that it can convert the instruction count of a statement into an integer plus instruction count. By measuring the times an integer plus instruction and, e.g., a double plus instruction consumes, we can approximate that in the period of time of one double plus instruction the CPU could have performed x integer plus instructions. For instance, we measure 5 nanoseconds for a double plus instruction and we measure 2 nanoseconds for an integer plus instruction. Then, in the time where one double plus instruction took place 2.5 integer plus instructions could have been performed.

3.4.2 Derivation

For derivation of the weights, we utilize the same approach which was described in Section 3.2 for MIPIPS. Instead of running a MIPIPS counter, the approach calculates the mega instructions per second for each statement, e.g. for double minus.

```java
int x = 0;
double y = 0.0;

long startTime = System.currentTimeMillis();

int i = -2147483647;
while (i < 2147483647) {
  x = x + 2;
  y = y - 3.0;
  i += 1;
}

long endTime = System.currentTimeMillis();
long difftime = endTime - startTime;
System.out.println(difftime);
System.out.println(x);
System.out.println(y);
```

Listing 16: Double minus weight benchmark in Java

Afterwards, it divides the MIPIPS value by the corresponding mega instructions per second for each statement.

Listing 16 lists an example for calculating the mega instructions per second for a double minus statement in Java. It equals the MIPIPS counter except that line 2 declares y as a double and in line 9 y is subtracted by 3. Like the MIPIPS, the runtime of the weight benchmark is measured and with the runtime of the calibration run mega double plus instruction per second (MDMIPS) are calculated. For example, we assume MIPIPS to be 200 and MDMIPS to be 50. Thus, the weight for double minus is $200/50 = 4$.

Our benchmark program contains a set of weight benchmarks for most used statements. These are integer, float, double, long and for each the operations plus, minus, divide, multiply. Furthermore, benchmarks for boolean and, boolean or, boolean not, class creation, field access, function call, and String plus are available. Table 3 shows an overview of the contained weight benchmarks. More weight benchmarks can be added by creating language independent instances of our class definition meta-model to the benchmark generator and using Xpand for the generation of the source code.

3.5 Network Traffic

This section describes the derivation of the quantity of network traffic between nodes.

Data type	Operations
Integer	plus, minus, divide, multiply
Float	plus, minus, divide, multiply
Double	plus, minus, divide, multiply
Long	plus, minus, divide, multiply
Boolean	and, or, not
Internal	class creation, field access, function call
String	plus

Table 3: Contained weight benchmarks

```
1  class Class1 {
2    private int attrib1 = 0;
3    private Class2 attrib2 = new Class2();
4  }
5
6  public Class2 {
7    private int attrib3 = 3;
8  }
```

Listing 17: Example of determining the size of a class

3.5.1 Description

If methods are called on other nodes, they produce network traffic through the parameters that must be serialized and sent. We want to simulate the network traffic between nodes because it adds to the costs of a simulated run. Therefore, we need the size of types that are sent over the network. Primitive types are looked up in a language dependent size table. The size of a class has to be derived which is described in the following section.

3.5.2 Derivation

A static approach for the derivation of the size of a class is counting the size of the attributes of the class. Each attribute, that is declared as a primitive type, is counted with the value from a language dependent size table. If an attribute has the type of a class, the class is counted first. The counted attributes are summed up and this value forms the size of the class in bytes.

Listing 17 shows an example. The type size for *Class1* shall be determined. Therefore, its attributes are counted. *attrib1* is a primitive type and we assume that the language dependent table contains 4 bytes as the value for integers. *attrib2* has the type *Class2* and thus the size of *Class2* must be counted first. The size of *Class2* is 4 bytes because it only contains *attrib3* which is of the type integer. Summing up, *Class1* has the size $4 + 4 = 8$ bytes.

Considering a dynamic analysis, the derivation can, for instance, be conducted with a Kieker probe that determines the size of the parameters for the called method.

3.6 SMM Workload Profile

This section describes the components of an SMM workload profile and which types of SMM workload profiles are provided by CloudMIG Xpress.

3.6.1 Description

We need a workload profile that describes the usage model of the system that should be simulated. During simulation, Cloudlets are created from it. Therefore, a workload profile should contain a set of measurements. A single measurement should include the measurement timestamp, the measured response time, and the method that was measured. SMM provides an easy way to include those attributes.

3.6.2 Derivation

CloudMIG Xpress provides two different types of SMM workload profile. The first is a synthetic SMM workload profile. The user can create synthetic SMM workload profiles by specifying a workload function and other parameters like the associated method. Alternatively, the user can create an SMM workload profile by importing monitoring data from a dynamic analysis. Currently, CloudMIG Xpress supports importing monitoring data from Kieker traces.

3.7 Enriched KDM Model

A further input is an enriched KDM model which is described in this section.

3.7.1 Description

The KDM model contains a representation of the source code. The enrichments include a mapping between source code elements and *cloud code models*, and information about the cloud provider that the simulation should be conducted with. *Cloud code models* represent a logical composition of source code elements in the context of a specific cloud deployment option.

3.7.2 Derivation

The enriched KDM model is provided by CloudMIG Xpress.

3.8 Adaptation Rules

This section describes the input adaptation rules.

3.8.1 Description

Adaptation rules are required for starting and terminating instances on the basis of occurring events or thresholds. An example for an adaptation rule is "start a new virtual machine instance when for 60 seconds the average CPU utilization of allocated nodes stays above 70 %." The rules follow the reconfiguration model of CloudMIG Xpress and have the form of an action, i.e., start or terminate, a scope, i.e., all or only specific allocated nodes, a time period like 60 seconds, an utilization field like 70 %, and a relation like above or below.

3.8.2 Derivation

The user of CloudMIG Xpress creates the adaption rules using the GUI.

3.9 Configuration

In this section the simulation configuration parameters are specified and described.

3.9.1 Description

Parameter	Data type
Timeout	Double
Instruction counting method	Enumeration{dynamic, static, hybrid}
Approximate array size	Integer
Runtime of unknown methods	Double
Separate submethod mode	Boolean

Table 4: Simulation configuration parameters

Table 4 shows an overview of the simulation configuration parameters and their data types. The first parameter is the *timeout* for Cloudlets. Its data type is double in order to model arbitrary times. The *instruction counting method* parameter specifies, which approach for instruction counting should be used by the simulation. The three approaches were described in Section 3.3. The parameter *approximate array size* is used for determining the iteration count in the static approach when the iteration count cannot be derived. When the source code of a called method is not available in the static approach, the parameter *runtime of unknown methods* provides an approximation of the runtime. Its data type is double to model arbitrary runtimes. The separate submethod mode is described in detail in Section 5.12.

3.9.2 Derivation

The user of CloudMIG Xpress provides the configuration by defining values for them using the GUI.

4 Simulation Output

This section describes the output of the simulation. Sections 4.1 to 4.3 describe the different output components. The outputs for different cloud deployment options have to be comparable to propose which deployment option is more suitable. Hence, we describe our rating approach in Section 4.4. Elasticity is a further output that we plan to integrate as a future feature. How elasticity can be measured is described in Section 9.6.

4.1 Costs

The first output of the simulation are the costs of the simulated cloud deployment option. It represents an overall cost which is the sum of the costs for the used bandwidth and virtual machine instances. The overall cost is the primary attribute of this category that is incorporated in the overall rating.

For example, assume one virtual machine instance running for 23 hours and one virtual machine instance running for 6 hours. Furthermore, the costs for running one virtual machine instance is assumed with 0.095\$ per hour. Then, the output for the costs is $23 \cdot 0.095\$ + 6 \cdot 0.095\$ = 2.755\$$.

4.2 Response Times

Another output of the simulation is the median of the response times for each called method. Each method is then rated by our rating approach. Based on the method ratings, an overall rating for the response times is calculated. This overall rating for the response times is the primary attribute that is included in the overall rating.

4.3 SLA Violations

The third output is the number of violations for each SLA. Currently, only the SLA "a call will not timeout" is implemented. The GUI provides the possibility to change the timeout value. However, we plan to support a generic definition and processing of SLAs.

4.4 Rating

For comparing different simulation runs that cover different cloud deployment options, we do a rating for each run. The rating scale ranges from 1 as the best to 5 as the worst performance. Our rating approach searches for the best performance of all runs in each category and sets this performance as a 1. The same is done for the worst performance and the corresponding run is set as a 5. The other runs are rated relatively to the best and worst run with the following method. The median of all runs is calculated and set as a 3. The median divides the runs into a left set and a right set, where the values that already got a rate are not included. The left set is taken, the median is calculated, and then set as a 2. The same is done for the right set and the median is set as a 4. After this, the values that have not been associated to a rating, are members of four groups, namely the group between 1 and 2, between 2 and 3, between 3 and 4, and between 4 and 5. These members are assigned a rating according to linear approximation. If there is only one run, the rating is 1. The algorithm for the rating approach is shown in Appendix D.

For example, assuming the six runs with the costs of 10\$, 20\$, 40\$, 50\$, 90\$, and 100\$. The 10\$ run is rated as 1 and the 100\$ run is rated as a 5. Then the median of the set is calculated which is 45\$, which would be the value for a 3. The left set contains 20\$ and 40\$ and the right set contains 50\$ and 90\$. The median of the left set is 30\$ which is the value for a 2 and the median of the right set is 70\$ which is the value for a 4. 20\$ gets the rating 1.5. 40\$ gets the rating 2.66. 50\$ gets the rating 3.2. 90\$ gets the rating 4.66.

The overall rating, that considers each output, forms a combined rating by multiplying the output rating with a weight, summing the resulting values, and rounding it at the second decimal place. It can be configured which output is more important by specifying other weights than the default weight of 0.33 for each output rating.

5 CloudSim Enhancements

Section 5.1 provides an overview of our enhancements to CloudSim. Then, Section 5.2 shows the enhanced CloudSim meta-model. Finally, Sections 5.3 to 5.12 describe the accomplished extensions to CloudSim.

5.1 Overview

CloudSim simulates cloud systems following a cloud provider perspective. However, we require the cloud user perspective for the simulation of cloud deployment options. For a cloud provider the workload on the nodes is rather random in general. Therefore, we needed to implement a CPU utilization model that is not basing on randomness (see Section 5.3). Furthermore, CloudSim provides no comfortable way of conditionally starting and terminating virtual machine instances at runtime. Hence, we implemented a rule-based system for this purpose which we describe in Section 5.4. In CloudSim, all Cloudlets start processing at the beginning of the simulation. However, we need an easy way of specifying a start time of a Cloudlet (see Section 5.5). The initialization time of virtual machine instances is most often not negligible. Hence, we implemented a delayed virtual machine instance start which is further described in Section 5.6. In most real systems, requests can timeout. We model this circumstance with a configurable timeout for Cloudlets (see Section 5.7). CloudSim only provides a very basic debt model. For advanced debt modeling, we improved the debt model (see Section 5.8). In addition, we enhanced the modeling of the instruction count of Cloudlets (see Section 5.9). Section 5.10 presents our history exporter for easier traceability of conducted simulations. In order to have a virtual unlimited amount of virtual machine instances, we needed dynamic host addition at runtime which is described in Section 5.11. Our new Cloudlet scheduler is presented in Section 5.12.

5.2 Enhanced CloudSim Meta-Model

Figure 8 displays the enhanced CloudSim meta-model. The enhancements are marked with a gray background. Here, we only describe the enhancements. The rest of the diagram was already described in paragraph 2.2.1. We added classes for representing the network price function for each datacenter, i.e., *NetworkPrice* and *NetworkStepPrice*. In addition, the virtual machine instance price is modeled by the class *VMInstancePrice*. Those three classes are part of the improved debt model

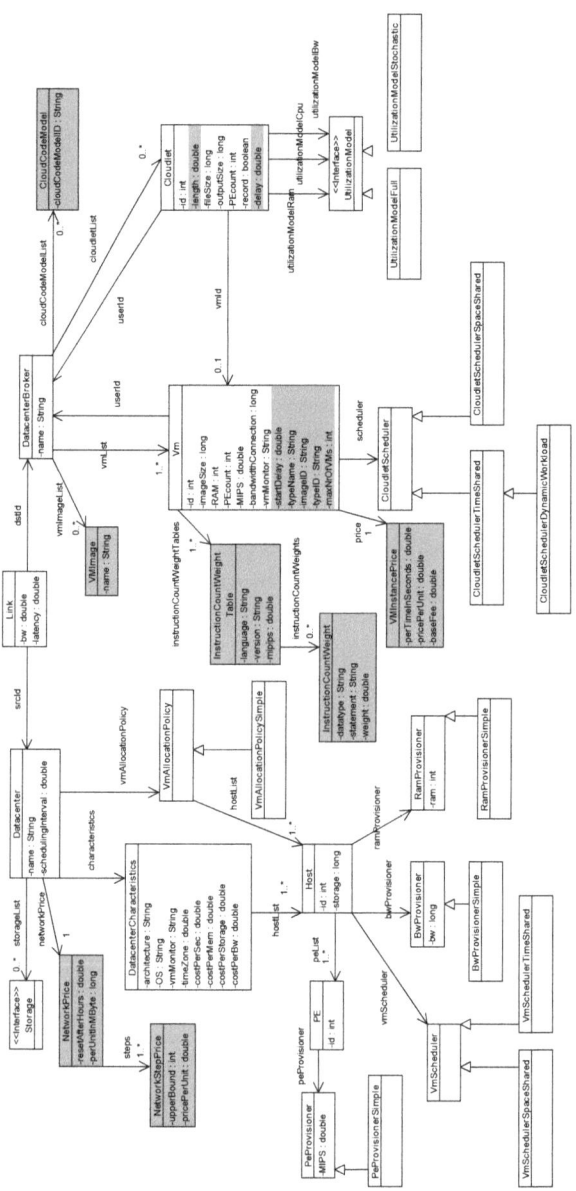

Figure 8: Enhanced CloudSim meta-model

which is described in Section 5.8. In order to support the improved instruction count model (see Section 5.9), we had to change the data type of the attribute *length* from the *Cloudlet* class to double. For delayed Cloudlet sending (see Section 5.5), we added the attribute *delay* to the class *Cloudlet*. The new classes *VMImage* and *CloudCodeModel* and the new attributes *typeName*, *imageID*, *typeID*, and *maxNrOfVMs* of the class *Vm* are used for the creation and termination of virtual machine instances which is described in Section 5.4. Furthermore, the static approach utilizes the two new classes *InstructionCountWeightTable* and *InstructionCountWeight*. We added the new attribute *startDelay* to the class *Vm* for the delayed virtual machine instance creation which is described in Section 5.6.

5.3 CPU Utilization Model per Core

CloudSim only provides a pure random-based CPU utilization model because the CPU utilization is rather random for a cloud provider. However, from the cloud user perspective we know the approximate CPU utilization and it is a major predictor indicator for the performance of the virtual machine instance. Hence, we implemented a CPU utilization model that follows the conducted work. Our CPU utilization model is motivated by the fact that a 50 % CPU utilization in one second means that the CPU had work in 500 milliseconds and was idle in 500 milliseconds.

Figure 9 shows an example. The gray boxes indicate when the CPU was active. From 0 to 0.22 seconds and 0.43 to 0.72 seconds the CPU was working. From 0.23 to 0.42 seconds and from 0.73 to 1.0 seconds the CPU was idle. Our CPU utilization model only queries at discrete timestamps whether the CPU is active or idle. In Figure 9, the queries for the CPU utilization are sketched by the vertical lines at each 0.1 seconds. Notably, our CPU utilization model has a discretization error and we can construct cases where the actual CPU utilization is 99 % and the CPU utilization in our model is 0 %. However, our tests have shown that the error of our CPU utilization model is negligible for most workloads. The CPU utilization model in our simulation queries the CPU action every 10 milliseconds in simulation time.

5.4 Starting and Stopping Virtual Machine Instances on Demand

In CloudSim the virtual machine instances cannot be started on demand. They have to be created before the simulation begins. Hence, there is no possibility to simulate automatic elasticity in CloudSim. The CloudSim authors provide a way to stop the

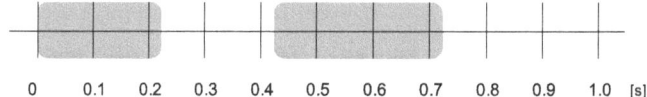

Figure 9: CPU utilization model example

simulation and then change the configuration. However, using this way for elasticity would mean that we stop the simulation each minute and test if the configuration must be changed. This activity should be an internal function and as cloud users we should only need to define adaptation rules. We implemented this feature into CloudSim. The adaptation rules were described in Section 3.8.

5.5 Delayed Cloudlet Creation

CloudSim needs all Cloudlets to be started at the beginning, if we ignore the intractable method of stopping the simulation at a defined timestamp. With this behavior web applications cannot be modeled in a realistic way because all requests would be at the beginning of the simulation and parallel. Hence, we extended CloudSim such that Cloudlets have an attribute *delay* which corresponds to the time when the Cloudlet should be sent for processing.

5.6 Delayed Start of Virtual Machines

In CloudSim a creation of a virtual machine results in instant availability of the virtual machine instance. Our conducted tests showed that, for example, there is an average delay of one minute on our private cloud which is not negligible. Therefore, we implemented an event for the delayed creation of virtual machines. The old creation method is triggered from this event.

5.7 Timeout for Cloudlets

In web applications there is typically a response timeout. After this timeout, an answer is useless because the client closed the connection. Most real web applications would recognize when a user closes the connection by timeout and would terminate the corresponding task that calculates the answer. This results in a saving of CPU time. Hence, we also implemented a timeout for calls. Every Cloudlet that is executing, paused, or waiting, gets canceled after a defined timeout.

5.8 Improved Debt Model

The debt model in CloudSim is kept coarse grained. In particular, our tests have shown that it counts the used memory and bandwidth, multiplies these with a constant, and returns the resulting value. Modeling the current debt model of Amazon EC2 is not possible with this debt model. Hence, we implemented a debt model that follows the pricing model of CloudMIG Xpress and takes a time span for which the debts are calculated. For instance, for modeling the virtual machine instance debt model of Amazon EC2 every begun hour the price for the running instance is added to the debts. Furthermore, the debt model for bandwidth usage is modeled as a step function like done by Amazon EC2. For example, the first gigabyte of traffic is free of charge, above one gigabyte till 10,000 gigabyte every gigabyte costs 0.12$ at the time of this writing.

5.9 Enhanced Instruction Count Model

Cloudlets in CloudSim have an attribute called *length* with the data type long. This length is assumed to be in mega instructions. Assuming, for instance, a MIPIPS of 200, the shortest execution of a Cloudlet that can be modeled is five milliseconds. In the web application domain this value might be too high. We wanted to model also short calls. Therefore, we changed the data type to double and hence, enabled a modeling of arbitrary small call durations.

5.10 History Exporter

CloudSim only has a function for recording the actions of Cloudlets as a String. These actions include starting and finishing, for instance. All other events are logged, but only on the console for a human user. We extended CloudSim by a history exporter for the CPU utilizations, arrival rates, and response times. The CPU utilizations are written on a per core basis. The arrival rates and response times are written on a per method basis. After exporting, the resulting CSV files can be read in by an included R script and plotted such that the run of the simulation is easily traceable.

5.11 Dynamic Host Addition at Runtime

In a Cloud environment like Amazon EC2, a virtually unlimited amount of virtual machine instances can be started. Modeling this circumstance with CloudSim would mean that we must limit the amount because we can only add a limited amount of hosts upfront. We made an extension to CloudSim that with every virtual machine instance a new host, that fits the needs of the virtual machine instance, is added dynamically at runtime.

5.12 Method Calls and Network Traffic between Virtual Machine Instances

In CloudSim, a Cloudlet runs on one virtual machine instance and it can be moved to other virtual machine instances but a Cloudlet cannot "call" other Cloudlets.

We wanted to simulate the explicit calling of methods between different virtual machine instances and on the same instance. We call this *separate submethods mode (S2M)*. For example, a use case for this is the calling of web services on other virtual machine instances. For this purpose, we had to implement a new Cloudlet scheduler. Figure 10 shows an example for the new scheduler. There exists *method1* which should execute on *VM1* and should call *method2* on *VM2*. *Method1* is represented by *Cloudlet1*. Before *Cloudlet1* is executed, the scheduler searches in the source code of *method1* for methods that are called by *method1*. A call to *method2* is found and the *Index Service* is queried for the location where *method2* is running. The *Index Service* returns *VM2* and for *method2 Cloudlet2* is created on *VM2*. Then, *Cloudlet1* pauses itself, meaning other Cloudlets can process on *VM1*. *Method2* conducts no method calls. Therefore, *Cloudlet2* processes and then wakes up *Cloudlet1* on finish. *Cloudlet1* can now process or call other methods.

The previously mentioned *Index Service* tracks which method is available on which virtual machine instance. This service also implements a basic load balancer on a per method basis. It saves an index and outputs the different virtual machine instances circularly.

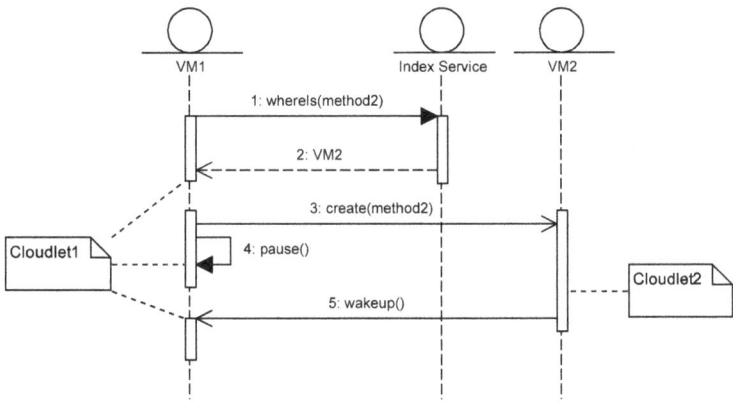

Figure 10: New scheduling example

6 MIPIPS and Weights Benchmark

We implemented our approach for the derivation of MIPIPS (see Section 3.2) and weights (see Section 3.4) as a benchmark software in Java. Section 6.1 provides a list of the main features and Section 6.2 presents the design of the software. Finally, Section 6.3 shows an example of the output.

6.1 Features

The purpose of the MIPIPS and weights benchmark is the determination of MIPIPS and weights for different programming languages. It provides the following main features:

- Determination of MIPIPS and weights for different programming languages

- Configuration of which programming language to benchmark and the number of runs for measuring MIPIPS and weights

- Interaction through the Console or GUI

- Output the results as a CSV file

6.2 Design

The design of the MIPIPS and weights benchmark follows the Model-View-Controller (MVC) design pattern, i.e., the software is separated into logic, model, and view.

In Figure 11, the Java packages for the MIPIPS and weights benchmark are displayed. The package *mipipsandweightscounter* contains the logic that implements the master which starts the single benchmarks. *mipipsandweightscounter.console* and *mipipsandweightscounter.view* provide the console and graphical user interface. The package *mipipsandweightscounter.command* includes classes for starting the single benchmarks.

In Figure 12, the GUI of the MIPIPS and weights benchmark is shown. The left part enables the configuration of the benchmark and provides a start button for the benchmark. Furthermore, the lower left part displays information about the last benchmark run. The right part of the GUI is used for showing logging events.

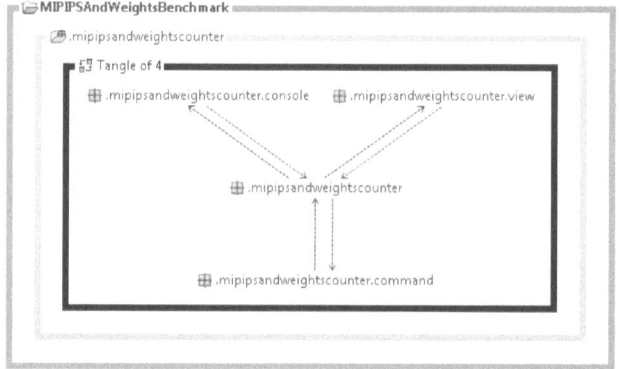

Figure 11: Java packages of the MIPIPS and weights benchmark

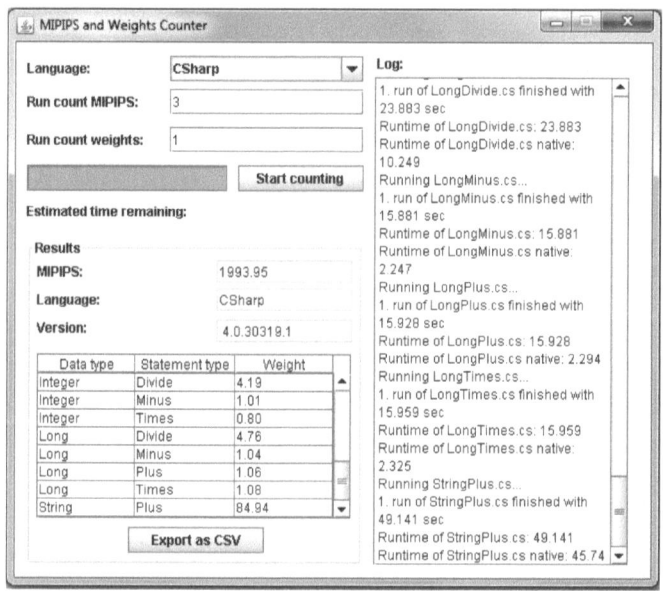

Figure 12: GUI of the MIPIPS and weights benchmark

```
 1  #MIPIPS = 1993.949533426184
 2  #Language = CSharp
 3  #Version = 4.0.30319.1
 4  #Datatype, Statementtype, Weight
 5  Boolean, And, 0.8546889507892294
 6  Boolean, Not, 3.505571030640669
 7  Boolean, Or, 0.9419684308263695
 8  Class, Creation, 16.77251622931359
 9  Double, Divide, 19.76462395543176
10  Double, Minus, 2.846332404828227
11  Double, Plus, 2.9986072423398324
12  Double, Times, 2.976787372330548
13  Field, Access, 1.0649953574744664
14  Float, Divide, 17.055710306406688
15  Float, Minus, 2.8681522748375117
16  Float, Plus, 2.6727019498607243
17  Float, Times, 2.904363974001857
18  Function, Call, 2.2307335190343545
19  Integer, Divide, 4.1861652739090065
20  Integer, Minus, 1.0069637883008358
21  Integer, Times, 0.8040854224698235
22  Long, Divide, 4.758124419684309
23  Long, Minus, 1.043175487465181
24  Long, Plus, 1.0649953574744664
25  Long, Times, 1.0793871866295266
26  String, Plus, 84.93964706917666
```

Listing 18: Example output of the MIPIPS and weights benchmark

6.3 Example Output

Listing 18 shows an example output of the MIPIPS and weights benchmark. The first line contains the measured MIPIPS. Then, line 2 and 3 determine the language and the corresponding version. Afterwards, the weights are displayed in the form: data type, statement type, and weight.

7 CDOSim

CDOSim is a software, which we developed within the scope of this thesis to enable the simulation of different cloud deployment options. We implemented CDOSim as a plug-in for ClougMIG Xpress [18]. The source code is available on the attached DVD. The future work for CDOSim is described in Section 10.2. Section 7.1 and 7.3 show an overview of the features and the design of CDOSim and Section 7.2 presents the fundamental activities that are performed by CDOSim during the simulation.

7.1 Features

CDOSim enables the simulation of different cloud deployment options. Currently, the following main features are implemented:

- Simulation of software systems in the context of CloudMIG's cloud profiles

- Simulation of costs, response times, and SLA violations

- Simulation of software systems that were reverse-engineered to KDM code models

- Simulation of SMM models that represent workload profiles and enrich KDM models

- Start or shutdown of virtual machine instances based on the average CPU utilization of allocated virtual machine instances corresponding to arbitrary workload patterns

- Configurable timeout for service calls

- Export of runs as CSV files for CPU utilization, response times, and arrival rate

- Configuration of the start instance type and how many instances are running at start

- Integration of adaptation rules and pricing package from CloudMIG Xpress

For the planned features, we refer to the description of the future work in Section 10.2.

7.2 The Simulation Process

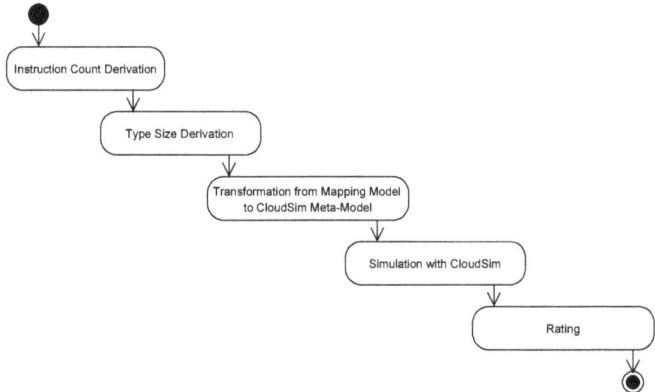

Figure 13: Activities in CDOSim's simulation process

Figure 13 shows the different activities performed by CDOSim during simulation. The first activity is *instruction count derivation*. In this activity CDOSim conducts the instruction count derivation with the approach, which was selected by the user. The derived instruction counts are written as attributes into the KDM instances, that were passed to the simulation. Secondly, the type size is derived as described in Section 3.5. We need the type size to approximate the bandwidth that is used when there are distributed calls to other virtual machine instances. The next activity is the transformation from the mapping model provided by CloudMIG Xpress to our CloudSim Meta-Model. The mapping model contains the meta-information about, for instance, the available instance types and costs of the selected cloud provider. Furthermore, it describes which code models have to be deployed on specific virtual machine instances. Then, the actual *simulation with CloudSim* takes place. Finally, the new simulation result is rated relative to the other runs. In non-GUI mode, the runs, which should be ranked relatively, can be passed to CDOSim. The rating approach was described in Section 4.4.

7.3 Design

We designed CDOSim with the MVC design pattern, i.e., we separated the logic, model, and view. Furthermore, every activity (see Section 7.2) has its own package.

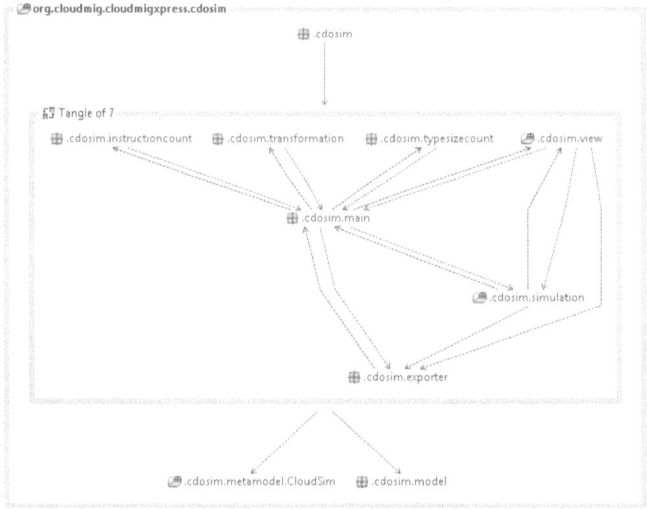

Figure 14: Java packages of CDOSim

In Figure 14 the Java packages of CDOSim are shown. The *cdosim* package contains an activator class which is called when the plug-in is started from within CloudMIG Xpress. The models, e.g., a class for the simulation results, are included in the *model* package. The CloudSim meta-model is contained in the *metamodel.CloudSim* package. The interface for CloudMIG Xpress is provided by the *main* package. Furthermore, it invokes the different activities which reside in their own package. These packages are *instructioncount*, *typesizecount*, *transformation*, and *simulation*. The *view* package is responsible for displaying the GUI and the *exporter* package is responsible for saving data like the CPU utilization during the simulation into CSV files.

Figure 15 shows the GUI of CDOSim. The GUI is divided into two parts. The upper part shows the configuration for the next simulation run and provides a button for starting the simulation. The lower part of the GUI displays the past simulation runs and their rated results.

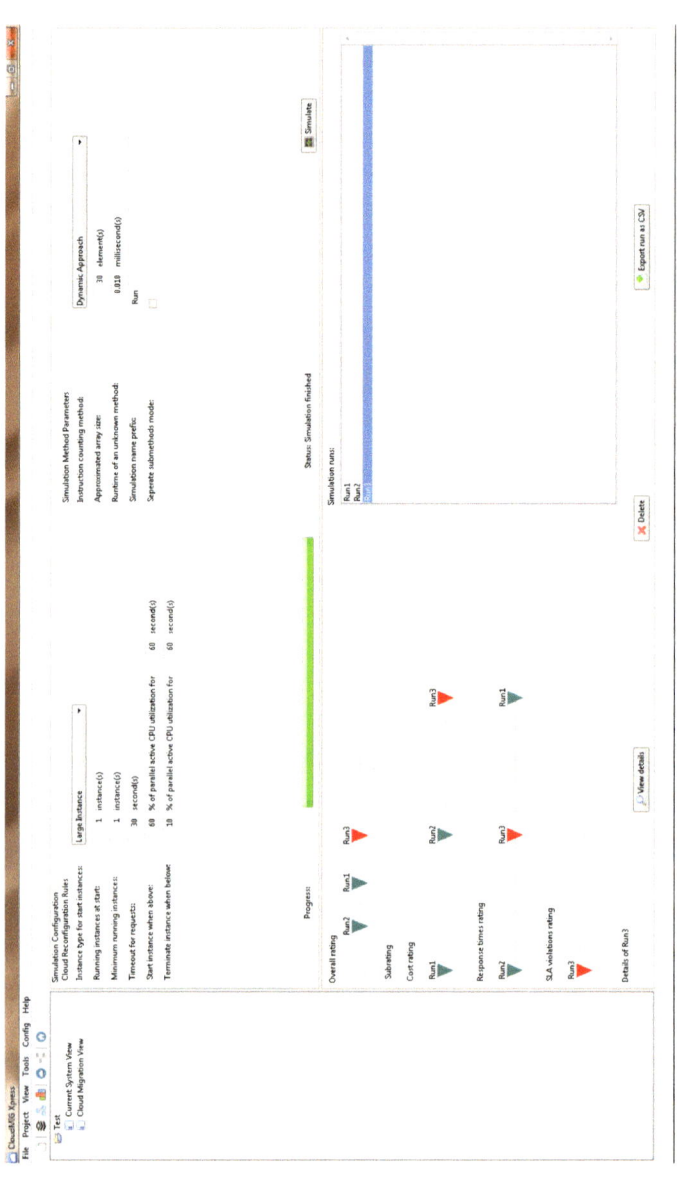

Figure 15: GUI of CDOSim

8 Evaluation of CDOSim

This section evaluates the functionality and accuracy of CDOSim. Furthermore, the MIPIPS benchmark is evaluated because it represents an important precondition for CDOSim. Section 8.1 describes the goals of the five different evaluations, which we refer to by E1 to E5, and the rationale for conducting them. Afterwards, Section 8.2 presents the methodology that we used in E1 to E5. In Section 8.3, the basic experiment setup for the different evaluations is described. Then, Sections 8.4 to 8.8 detail the conducted evaluations. Finally, Section 8.9 summarizes the results of the evaluations.

8.1 Goals of the Evaluation

E1, which is described in Section 8.4, evaluates the validity of the MIPIPS benchmark. The MIPIPS value should correlate with the performance that the underlying node provides. Furthermore, it should be approximately constant on the same node. The MIPIPS value is important when there is a run on one cloud provider or a local server, and we want to simulate which performance and costs the workload would induce on a specific cloud provider or cloud provider in general.

In E2 the validity of the simulation results in comparison to real, measured runs on Eucalyptus and Amazon EC2, that are conducted with single core instances, are evaluated. This evaluation is important to assess the basic validity of the simulation. In addition, it evaluates which simulation approach, that were described in Section 3, reveals the most accurate result.

E3 also evaluates the validity of the simulation by determining the accuracy of the simulation referred to the measured runs on Eucalyptus and Amazon EC2. However, E3 utilizes a multi core instance type instead of a single core instance type.

E4 evaluates whether the simulation accurately simulates a wider range of adaptation strategies.

Evaluation E5 combines E1, E2, and E3. It evaluates whether the prediction of the performance of a cloud provider basing on the data from another cloud provider is accurate, i.e., we do a run on Amazon EC2 with a multi core instance type and predict the performance of this workload on Eucalyptus with a single core instance type. Then, the run is conducted on Eucalyptus and compared to the simulated run. The MIPIPS values of the multi core instance type and the single core instance type are an important part of this evaluation. If they are wrong, the prediction will under- or overestimate the performance on Eucalyptus relative to the Amazon EC2 run.

Following the three types of validity for simulation models by Zeigler [56, 68, 69, 77], E2, E3, and E4 evaluate the replicative validity of our simulation model and E5 addresses the predictive and structural validity. A reproduction is in some way also a prediction. However, we refer to a prediction only if it corresponds to input values that are recorded on a different system than the system that should be simulated.

8.2 Methodology

This section describes our methodology used in the evaluations E1 to E5.

8.2.1 Comparison Method in E1

In evaluation E1, we want to show that the MIPIPS values stay approximately constant on the same node. Furthermore, the MIPIPS value should correlate with the performance that the underlying node provides, i.e, if there exists a large difference in other performance measures, it should be likely that the MIPIPS values express this circumstance.

For determining if the MIPIPS stay approximately constant on the same platform, we calculate the mean value and the standard deviation over the MIPIPS values resulting from the conducted runs. Then, we compare the standard deviation to a predefined threshold.

The correlation between the performance of the underlying host and the MIPIPS will be evaluated by comparing the MIPIPS with the available performance attribute and checking if the difference between the MIPIPS values is statistically significant.

8.2.2 Calculation of Relative Error for E2 to E5

For the evaluations E2 to E5 we compare the simulated values with the measured values per minute. The values are CPU utilization, instance count, costs, and response times. The following metric describes the relative error for each aspect of the simulation. All percent values will be truncated after the second decimal place.

T is the set of all minutes in the measurement duration. $m(t)$ is the measured value at timestamp $t \in T$ and $s(t)$ is the simulated value at timestamp $t \in T$. When $m(t)$ equals 0, t is removed from the set T. Equation 9 shows the formula to calculate the relative error for a timestamp t.

(9) $$re(t) = \frac{|m(t) - s(t)|}{m(t)}, \ m(t) \neq 0, \ t \in T$$

(10) $$RE = \frac{\Sigma_t \ re(t)}{|T|}$$

Equation 10 displays the formula for calculation of the relative error (RE) for the whole simulation run. We have four different REs. RE_{CPU} is the relative error of the CPU utilization. $RE_{InstanceCount}$ stands for the relative error of the instance count. RE_{Costs} marks the relative error of the costs output. RE_{RT} is the relative error of the response times.

(11) $$OverallRE = \frac{RE_{CPU} + RE_{InstanceCount} + RE_{Costs} + RE_{RT}}{4}$$

To enable a consolidated comparison between the results, we introduce the overall relative error (OverallRE), which is shown in Equation 11. The overall relative error ($OverallRE$) should be below 30 % to have results that are sufficiently accurate [37, 43].

As a further comparison value, the overall difference of instance minutes and absolute costs will be provided. Instance minutes is the sum of the runtime of all virtual machine instances in minutes. For example, two virtual machine instances are running for one minute. Then, they consumed two instance minutes.

8.3 Basic Experiment Setup

This section describes the common setup for our evaluations. We use iBatis JPetStore 5.0 [27] for the evaluations E2 to E5, which is a web store for pets. The program is widely used for evaluation purposes.

8.3.1 SLAstic and SLAstic Adaptations

The online-adaptation framework SLAstic [73] provides means for architectural runtime reconfiguration. It can change component deployments and server allocations at runtime according to defined metrics and thresholds.

We extended SLAstic to function with Amazon EC2 by implementing an interface provided by SLAstic. SLAstic can now start and terminate virtual machine instances automatically on Amazon EC2. Furthermore, we implemented a CPU utilization based adaptation strategy. When the average CPU utilization of all allocated nodes is constantly above a configurable threshold value for a configurable amount of time, SLAstic triggers the creation of a new instance. Conversely, if the average CPU utilization of all allocated nodes is below a configurable threshold, the program triggers the shutdown of a running instance.

8.3.2 JPetStore Adaptation

Most calls to JPetStore are processed in less than 2 milliseconds, which results in only a small CPU utilization. In our evaluation, we want to use capacity adaption based on CPU utilization. We could generate a high call rate such that the CPU utilization raises over our threshold value for the starting of a new virtual machine instance. However, we would need different servers to generate the necessary workload intensity. Hence, we decided to generate additional CPU utilization for each call. Listing 19 shows the method that generates the CPU utilization. This method is called by every service method before processing its actual code.

We did not implement data flow analysis in the *static approach*. However, we needed line 6 and 7 such that the JIT did not optimize the while loop. With those two lines in the *static approach* and without data flow analysis, the instruction count will be about 50 % larger. With data flow analysis, those two lines would only increase the instruction count by far below 1 %. Hence, we omitted line 6 and 7 in the evaluations with the *static approach* because they are negligible if we would have implemented data flow analysis.

8.3.3 Eucalyptus

First, the private cloud software Eucalyptus, which is deployed on our own server, is part of the evaluations. This way, we can control the overall workload intensity on the underlying hosts, which in contrast is not possible on Amazon EC2. This section describes our Eucalyptus server and the experiment setup concerning Eucalyptus.

Configuration

Table 5 presents the hardware configuration for our Eucalyptus server. The two AMD Opteron 2384 processors provide 8 CPU cores in sum. The server has 24 GB DDR2-667 RAM and a 1 Gigabit/s network connection.

```
 1  public final int compute() {
 2    int retVal = 0;
 3    int i = 0;
 4
 5    while (i < 12582912) {
 6      if (i == 0)
 7        retVal = new Random();
 8
 9      retVal = retVal + 2;
10      i++;
11    }
12
13    return retVal;
14  }
```

Listing 19: JPetStore adaptation

CPU	2x AMD Opteron 2384 with 2.7 GHz
RAM	24 GB DDR2-667
Network	1 Gigabit/s

Table 5: Our Eucalyptus server

Instance type	Maximum number of instances	CPU cores per instance	RAM per instance
m1.small	8	1	1 GB
c1.medium	8	1	2 GB
m1.xlarge	4	2	2 GB
m1.large	2	4	2 GB
c1.xlarge	1	6	2 GB

Table 6: Our Eucalyptus configuration

Table 6 shows the instance type configuration for our Eucalyptus setup. *m1.small* has a single CPU core and 1 GB RAM. *c1.medium* has likewise one CPU core and 2 GB RAM. Two CPU cores and 2 GB of RAM are assigned to *m1.xlarge*. *m1.large* features four CPU cores and 2 GB RAM. At last, *c1.xlarge* has the highest CPU core count with 6 CPU cores and has 2 GB RAM.

Deployment

Figure 16 shows the deployment of the used components in Eucalyptus. Our test environment incorporates two nodes, namely the Eucalyptus node and the blade2

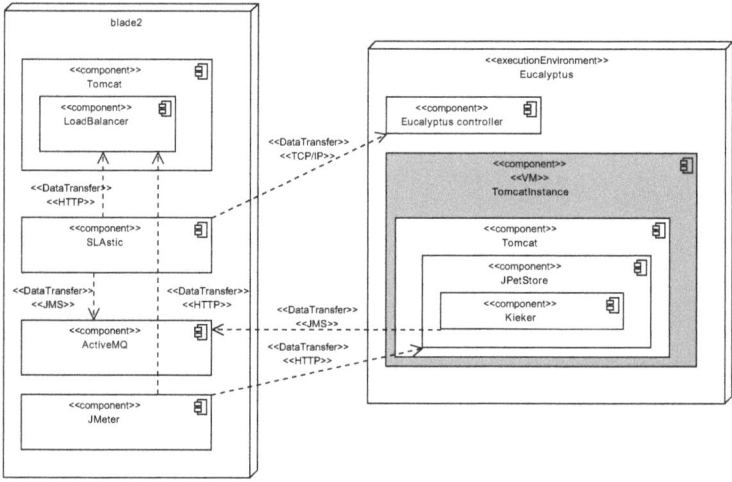

Figure 16: Deployment configuration for Eucalyptus

node. In the Eucalyptus node, instances of the Tomcat image can be started. The Tomcat image includes a Tomcat 6.0.18 [64] with JPetStore 5.0, its own database namely HSQLDB 1.8 [67], and Kieker 1.4 [70]. Kieker is included for monitoring the CPU utilization and response time of the annotated methods in JPetStore. It sends the monitored data to the ActiveMQ 5.5.1 [62] queue on the blade2 node. SLAstic 0.01a is deployed on the blade2 node. It analyzes the CPU utilization obtained from the ActiveMQ queue and calculates if a new instance of the Tomcat image should be allocated or if an instance can be released. If this circumstance holds, it communicates with the controller of Eucalyptus. The workload is generated by JMeter 2.5.1 [63] with Markov4JMeter [71] on the blade2 node. The JMeter profile fetches the destination IPs from the load balancer servlet at the start of a new web application call. The load balancer servlet manages a list that tracks virtual machine instances of the Tomcat image and passes a random IP to JMeter. SLAstic updates the server list.

Cost Model

Our Eucalyptus configuration has no cost model because it is a private cloud. Thus, we assume the cost model of Amazon EC2 EU (Irland) that applies at the time of this writing. We only list the used instance types. We assume for *m1.small* the costs of 0.095$ per started hour and for *m1.xlarge*, which is comparable to *c1.medium* from Amazon EC2, 0.19$ per started hour.

Cloud Profile

To simulate our Eucalyptus private cloud, we had to create a cloud profile for it in CloudMIG Xpress.

8.3.4 Amazon EC2

In addition to Eucalyptus, we conduct our evaluations on Amazon EC2 to include a realistic cloud environment that is widely used in industrial production settings. As with most public cloud providers, we can not control the workload intensity of the underlying host and which particular host we are spawning instances on. This section describes the specific deployment configuration for our evaluations done with Amazon EC2.

Used instance types

Instance type	CPU cores per instance	EC2 compute units per core	RAM per instance
t1.micro	1	Up to 2	613 MB
m1.small	1	1	1.7 GB
m1.large	2	2	7.5 GB
c1.medium	2	2.5	1.7 GB
m2.xlarge	2	3.25	17.1 GB

Table 7: Used instance types in Amazon EC2 experiments

Table 7 shows the used instance type configuration in our Amazon EC2 experiments. One EC2 compute unit provides the computing performance of a 1.0 to 1.2 GHz Opteron or Xeon processor from the year 2007. *t1.micro* has a single CPU core, up to 2 EC2 compute units, and 613 MB RAM. *m1.small* has a single CPU core, one EC2 compute unit, and 1.7 GB RAM. *m1.large* has 2 CPU cores, 2 EC2 compute units, and 7.5 GB RAM. Two CPU cores and 1.7 GB of RAM are assigned to *c1.medium*. *m2.xlarge* features two CPU cores, 3.25 EC2 compute units, and 17.1 GB RAM.

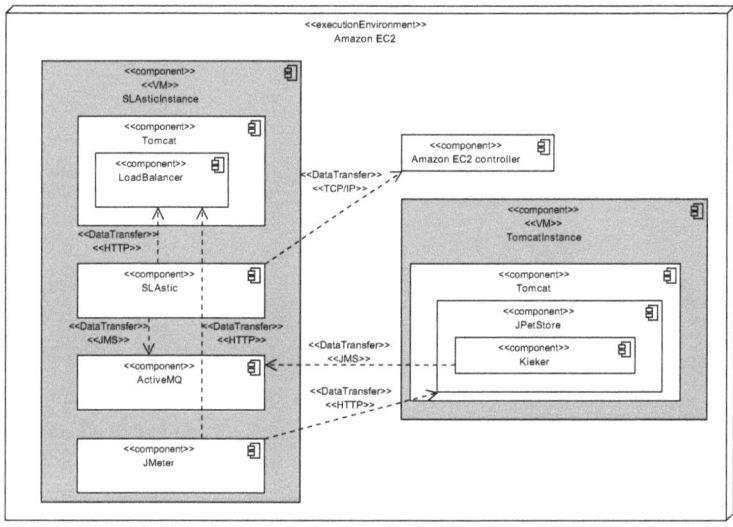

Figure 17: Deployment configuration for Amazon EC2

Deployment

Figure 17 shows the deployment for Amazon EC2. The communication types between the components are the same as in the Eucalyptus deployment. However, our server that is running SLAstic and the workload generator in Eucalyptus is not reachable from the Internet. Hence, we used an Amazon EC2 *m2.2xlarge* instance. This instance type has 34.2 GB RAM and 13 EC2 Compute Units (4 virtual cores with 3.25 EC2 Compute Units each).

Cost Model

We started all virtual machine instances in the region EU-West-1. Hence, we use the corresponding cost model. For a *m1.small* instance we payed 0.095$ per started hour and for a *c1.medium* instance we payed 0.19$ per started hour.

8.3.5 Workload Profile

Figure 18 presents the workload intensity function that is used in the evaluations E2 to E5. The workload intensity function origins from a service provider for digital photos [55]. It conforms to a typical day-night-cycle workload intensity often found

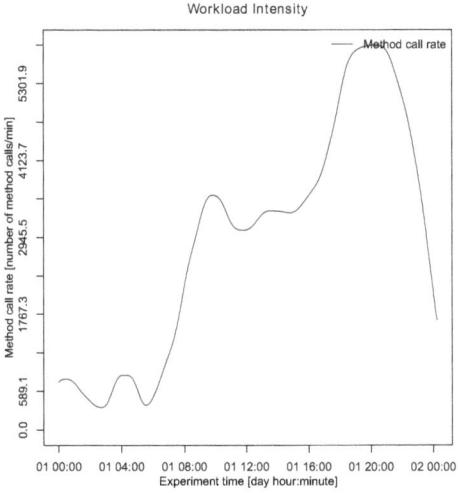

Figure 18: The used day-night-cycle workload intensity

on regional websites. In the morning the workload intensity increases until there is a first peak at noon and a second higher peak in the evening. Then, the workload intensity decreases until there are only few requests at night. The intensity of the used workload varies by each evaluation because our JMeter configuration takes a maximum value for the arrival rate at each minute but does not assert that this value is reached. The maximum value of the workload intensity for each evaluation E2 to E5 is described in the experiment setting of each evaluation. The evaluations E2 to E4 only reproduce the results and hence, the different workloads do not influence the results. In E5 the performance is predicted from a conducted run. Here, we conducted several runs for the control run to have approximately the same workload intensity.

8.3.6 Default Simulation Configuration

Table 8 shows the default simulation configuration for the evaluations E2 to E5. The configuration parameters were described in Section 3.9. If the value is not described in the evaluation, the value is set according to this table. The default value for *approximate array size* and *runtime of unknown methods* resulted from tests that performed best in this context. Further, they have a negligible influence

Setting	Value
Start instance type	m1.small
Running instances at start	1 instance
Minimum running instances	1 instance
Timeout	30 seconds
Start new instance when average CPU utilization	above 70 % for 60 seconds
Terminate instance when average CPU utilization	below 30 % for 60 seconds
Instruction counting method	dynamic approach
Approximate array size	30 elements
Runtime of unknown methods	0.01 milliseconds
Separate submethod mode	off

Table 8: Default simulation configuration

because JPetStore has only short service calls and only these are influenced by the two parameters. The largest part of the response time and work is produced by our JPetStore addition.

8.4 E1: MIPIPS Benchmark Evaluation

This section evaluates the MIPIPS benchmark. Section 8.4.1 to 8.4.6 describe the experiment and its results, discuss the results, and show the threats to validity.

8.4.1 Goals

The goal is to evaluate the MIPIPS benchmark by considering the plausibility of the resulting MIPIPS values in comparison to each other (validation) and the stability of the resulting MIPIPS values using the same instance type (verification).

We expect that, if there is a large difference in the performance of the CPU, the MIPIPS value of the slower CPU is smaller than the MIPIPS value of the faster CPU. In addition, we expect the MIPIPS value differs from the mean MIPIPS value by a small factor, which is lower than 2.5 %, if the benchmark is run again on the same instance type. The 2.5 % are motivated by the typical alpha level of $\alpha = 0.05$.

8.4.2 Experimental Setting

The evaluation takes place on Eucalyptus and Amazon EC2. On Eucalyptus we use the instance types *m1.small*, *m1.xlarge*, *m1.large*, and *c1.large*. These instances differ in the number of cores. We use solely these instance types because the MIPIPS benchmark measures CPU performance and always needs around 3 MB of memory. Hence, we omit instance types that differ only in the memory amount.

The MIPIPS benchmark on Amazon EC2 is run on the instance types *t1.micro*, *m1.small*, *m1.large*, *c1.medium*, and *m2.xlarge*. These instance types are the types where the EC2 Compute Units differ. Again, we omit instance types that distinguish solely in memory amount. The instances are started in the region EU-West-1.

All benchmark runs are started with the parameters for console mode, Java as benchmarked language, and 30 passes for the MIPIPS determination.

8.4.3 Comparisons

The evaluation includes five comparisons. MIPIPS.1 and MIPIPS.3 compare the MIPIPS values between the different instance types and MIPIPS.2, MIPIPS.4, and MIPIPS.5 compare the MIPIPS values of repeated runs on identical instance types.

Comparison MIPIPS.1: Different Eucalyptus instance types

This comparison analyzes the relationship of MIPIPS values of different Eucalyptus instance types, which are generated by one benchmark run on each instance type. The corresponding instance is the only instance that is running on our Eucalyptus server while performing each benchmark run.

Comparison MIPIPS.2: Eucalyptus m1.small instance

MIPIPS.2 compares the MIPIPS values of an Eucalyptus *m1.small* instance for 5 runs. For every run, a new instance is started and only one instance is running on our Eucalyptus setup at a time.

Comparison MIPIPS.3: Different Amazon EC2 instance types

In this comparison, we compare the MIPIPS values of different Amazon EC2 instance types. Each benchmark is started only once for each instance type. The instances are started in parallel on Amazon EC2.

Comparison MIPIPS.4: Amazon EC2 m1.small instance

MIPIPS.4 analyzes the MIPIPS values of an Amazon EC2 *m1.small* instance for 5 runs. For every new benchmark run a new instance is started. The first run is taken from MIPIPS.3 and the other four instances are started in parallel on Amazon EC2.

Comparison MIPIPS.5: Amazon EC2 c1.medium instance

MIPIPS.5 has the same procedure like MIPIPS.4. However, the underlying instance type is *c1.medium* instead of *m1.small*.

8.4.4 Results

The following subsections describe the results of comparison MIPIPS.1 to MIPIPS.5.

Comparison MIPIPS.1

Eucalyptus instance type	MIPIPS	GHz per core	Cores
m1.small	217.19	2.7	1
m1.xlarge	192.10	2.7	2
m1.large	173.77	2.7	4
c1.large	155.84	2.7	6

Table 9: Results for comparison MIPIPS.1

In Table 9 the results for the comparison between the MIPIPS of different Eucalyptus instance types are displayed. The MIPIPS value for *m1.small* is the highest value with 217.19 MIPIPS in the comparison. It is followed by the *m1.xlarge* with 192.10 MIPIPS, which is a difference of 15.09 MIPIPS to *m1.small*. *m1.large* has a MIPIPS value of 173.77, resulting in a difference of 18.33 MIPIPS to *m1.xlarge*. The lowest MIPIPS value is 155.84 for *c1.large* and it differs by 17.93 MIPIPS to its predecessor.

Comparison MIPIPS.2

Run	MIPIPS
1	217.19
2	218.10
3	217.48
4	217.58
5	216.39

Table 10: Results for comparison MIPIPS.2

Table 10 shows the results for five runs of the MIPIPS benchmark on an Eucalyptus *m1.small* instance. The mean MIPIPS value of the five runs is 217.34 MIPIPS.

The standard deviation amounts to 0.62 MIPIPS. The highest absolute deviation from the mean is 0.95 MIPIPS, which is about 0.44 %.

Comparison MIPIPS.3

Amazon EC2 instance type	MIPIPS	EC2 compute units per core	Runtime of benchmark
t1.micro	4.11	up to 2	1,169.43 hours
m1.small	20.65	1	171.28 hours
m1.large	142.13	2	79.34 hours
c1.medium	148.81	2.5	52.89 hours
m2.xlarge	235.57	3.25	47.66 hours

Table 11: Results for comparison MIPIPS.3

Table 11 displays the results for MIPIPS.3. The *t1.micro* instance has the lowest MIPIPS value with 4.11 MIPIPS. The *m1.small* instance follows with 20.65 MIPIPS. Then, the *m1.large* instance comes with 142.13 MIPIPS. After the *m1.large* instance, the *c1.medium* instance has 148.81 MIPIPS. At last, the *m2.xlarge* instance has the highest MIPIPS value with 235.57 MIPIPS. The number of cores for each Amazon EC2 instance type are not shown in the table because in contrast to Eucalyptus we do not know the maximum number of cores that can be allocated on a physical node and how many cores are allocated at the physical node. Thus, it the showing of the number of cores would have no benefit.

Comparison MIPIPS.4

Run	MIPIPS	Runtime of benchmark
1	20.65	171.28 hours
2	62.34	123.91 hours
3	20.82	170.92 hours
4	62.46	124.29 hours
5	95.18	135.90 hours

Table 12: Results for comparison MIPIPS.4

The results for five runs of the MIPIPS benchmark on an Amazon EC2 *m1.small* instance are shown in Table 12. The mean MIPIPS value amounts to 52.29 MIPIPS and the standard deviation is 31.76 MIPIPS. The highest absolute MIPIPS value deviates from the mean by 42.89 MIPIPS, which is about 82.02 %. The consumed time by the benchmark decreases with higher MIPIPS, except in the fifth run where it is between the runs with 20 MIPIPS and 62 MIPIPS.

Comparison MIPIPS.5

Run	MIPIPS	Runtime of benchmark
1	148.81	52.89 hours
2	148.88	53.17 hours
3	150.05	52.73 hours
4	148.39	53.10 hours
5	148.19	52.26 hours

Table 13: Results for comparison MIPIPS.5

In Table 13 the results for five runs of the benchmark on an Amazon EC2 *c1.medium* instance are displayed. 148.86 MIPIPS is the mean MIPIPS value. The standard deviation equals 0.72 MIPIPS. The highest absolute deviation from the mean is 1.18 MIPIPS, which is about 0.8 %. The total runtimes of the benchmarks range from 52.26 hours to 53.17 hours.

8.4.5 Discussion of the Results

The following subsections discuss the results for the comparisons MIPIPS.1 to MIPIPS.5.

Comparison MIPIPS.1

The results show that the more cores are allocated on our Eucalyptus server, the less the MIPIPS value becomes. We had excepted that the MIPIPS values stays constant because the benchmark only runs on one single core and all other cores are idle. The decreasing performance on Eucalyptus, when more cores are allocated, suggests, that there is a considerable penalty for more allocated cores. However, if we assume that the more cores are allocated, the lower the performance gets, the results show that the MIPIPS values are plausible, i.e. they decrease. This assumption is not applicable to Amazon EC2 because we do not know how many cores are allocated on the underlying physical node.

Comparison MIPIPS.2

All MIPIPS values differ by at most 0.44 % from the mean value. This value is below our 2.5 % threshold and hence, the calculated MIPIPS value is approximately constant for an *m1.small* instance on Eucalyptus.

Comparison MIPIPS.3

From *m1.small* to *m2.xlarge*, the MIPIPS values increase and the EC2 Compute Units, that can be seen as a form of performance indicator, also increase. Thus, the MIPIPS benchmark produces plausible results for those instance types.

t1.micro is a special case. The full 2 EC2 Compute Units are only available, if there is free CPU time that can be used by the *t1.micro* instance. In our benchmark run, we observed that most CPU time (more than 90 %) is spent in steal mode. This mode represents the CPU time, where the hypervisor scheduled another instance for computing. Therefore, it is reasonable to assume that there were less than 1 EC2 Unit available to our *t1.micro* instance. Hence, the lower MIPIPS value in comparison to the *m1.small* instance is plausible.

Furthermore, the results show that the more MIPIPS, the less time the benchmark consumed. The decreasing of benchmark time is sufficient for a higher MIPIPS value but not necessary because we measure the difference between the calibration passes and the passes with the added integer plus statement. Therefore, the calibration run might have taken a longer time then it normally does and the MIPIPS counting run was faster than normally.

Comparison MIPIPS.4

The resulting MIPIPS values for each *m1.small* run deviate by at most 82.02 %, which is a large difference to our 2.5 % threshold. We attribute the large difference to the way *m1.small* instances are treated in Amazon EC2. While benchmarking, we observed that the CPU spends some arbitrary time in steal mode. Thus, the performance of the instance depends not negligible on the workload of other instances running on the host, which leads to no constant MIPIPS value. Thus, the results show that the performance of *m1.small* instances is non-deterministic from the cloud user perspective.

The fourth benchmark run took 124.29 hours and the fifth run took 135.90 hours, although the fourth run benchmarked less MIPIPS than the fifth run. Probably, while the calibration pass there was some workload on the host of the fifth run and in the measuring passes there was less workload on the host, resulting in a higher MIPIPS value but increased benchmark runtime.

Comparison MIPIPS.5

The MIPIPS values deviate by at most 0.8 % from the MIPIPS mean value and 0.8 % lies below our 2.5 % threshold. Therefore, the calculated MIPIPS value stays approximately constant for an *c1.medium* instance on Amazon EC2.

All benchmark runs consumed approximately the same time, which aligns with the approximately constant MIPIPS values.

8.4.6 Threats to Validity

Performing only one run in comparison MIPIPS.1 and MIPIPS.3 might have produced MIPIPS values that largely differ from the mean value, which would result by performing more runs. However, most MIPIPS results differ by more than 10 %, and the deviation for instances that negligibly depend on the workload intensity of other instances run on the same host was lower than 1 %. Thus, it is unlikely that those MIPIPS results are not valid. The *m1.large* and *c1.medium* instance types differ by 4 % in MIPIPS.3. Here, the measured value for *m1.large* might be by chance too small and thus a mean value for *m1.large* should be determined in future work.

On Amazon EC2, the performance of the instances can differ from the location where the virtual machine instances are spawned and how large the workload intensity on the running host is. For instance, Iosup et al. [29] showed this circumstance. Furthermore, the workload intensity on the node might have changed during the run [6]. We can not control these factors and thus, they stay as a threat to validity.

8.5 E2: Accuracy Evaluation for Single Core Instances

This section describes the accuracy evaluation for the simulation of single core instances.

8.5.1 Goals

The goal of this evaluation is the replicative validation of the simulation results by comparing the simulation results with the real cloud provider runs. Furthermore, the evaluation exams the different approaches that were described in Section 3 in respect to their relative error in comparison to the measured values.

We expect that in no S2M the *dynamic approach* achieves the most accurate results. In the S2M, the *dynamic approach* can not be applied because our test application, JPetStore, is not fully instrumented. Hence, the *hybrid approach* is assumed to be the most accurate approach.

8.5.2 Experimental Setting

The experiment setup was described in Section 8.3. For the Eucalyptus run, we use instance type *m1.small* and the maximal arrival rate amounts to 6,085 calls per minute. On Eucalyptus, *m1.small* has only one single core. For the Amazon EC2 run, we also use instance type *m1.small*. Here, the maximal arrival rate is 4,480 calls per minute and *m1.small* also has just one single core. Both runs start with one instance, which will not be terminated.

8.5.3 Scenarios

The evaluation includes eight scenarios. The *hybrid approach* in no S2M is omitted because in this mode it behaves like the *dynamic approach*. The *dynamic approach* in S2M is excluded because one precondition for it is not satisfied. The unsatisfied precondition is that not all methods are monitored and thus response times are not available for all methods.

Scenario SingleCore.1: Dynamic approach in no S2M for Eucalyptus run with m1.small

The workload from a run, that is conducted on Eucalyptus with *m1.small*, is taken and on the basis of it, the simulation takes place. The simulation is configured to use the *dynamic approach* and to not simulate separate submethod calls.

Scenario SingleCore.2: Static approach in no S2M for Eucalyptus run with m1.small

This is the same scenario like SingleCore.1 except that it uses the *static approach*.

Scenario SingleCore.3: Static approach in S2M for Eucalyptus run with m1.small

This is the same scenario like SingleCore.1 except that it uses the *static approach* and the simulation is configured to simulate separate submethod calls.

Scenario SingleCore.4: Hybrid approach in S2M for Eucalyptus run with m1.small

This is the same scenario like SingleCore.1 except that it uses the *hybrid approach* and the simulation is configured to simulate separate submethod calls.

Scenario SingleCore.5: Dynamic approach in no S2M for Amazon EC2 run with m1.small

The simulation takes place on the basis of the workload from a run, that is conducted on Amazon EC2 with *m1.small*. The simulation is configured to use the *dynamic approach* and to not simulate separate submethod calls.

Scenario SingleCore.6: Static approach in no S2M for Amazon EC2 run with m1.small

This is the same scenario like SingleCore.5 except that it uses the *static approach*.

Scenario SingleCore.7: Static approach in S2M for Amazon EC2 run with m1.small

This is the same scenario like SingleCore.5 except that it uses the *static approach* and the simulation is configured to simulate separate submethod calls.

Scenario SingleCore.8: Hybrid approach in S2M for Amazon EC2 run with m1.small

This is the same scenario like SingleCore.5 except that it uses the *hybrid approach* and the simulation is configured to simulate separate submethod calls.

8.5.4 Results

The following subsections describe the results of scenario SingleCore.1 to SingleCore.8. Every figure includes the measured values and the simulated values for easier comparison. For reasons of simplicity, only the major differences between the measured and simulated values are described. The response times are displayed for the method *addItemToCart* from *com.ibatis.jpetstore.presentation.CartBean* because in contrast to other classes, the *addItemToCart* class does not depend on the input and thus the response times produced by the variation of the CPU utilization can be seen clearer.

Scenario SingleCore.1

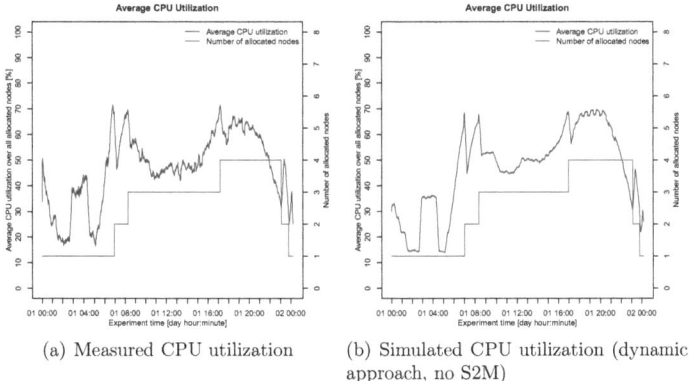

(a) Measured CPU utilization

(b) Simulated CPU utilization (dynamic approach, no S2M)

Figure 19: Average CPU utilization of allocated nodes in SingleCore.1 experiment

Figure 19 displays the average CPU utilization of the allocated nodes and the instance count for SingleCore.1 utilizing the *dynamic approach* in no S2M. The first peak at the beginning has a lower CPU utilization in the simulated run. The rest of the experiment time, the simulation and the conducted run are roughly equal or only deviate by below 5 % CPU utilization. The instance count is approximately the same between the conducted run and the simulation.

The relative error for the CPU utilization is $RE_{CPU} = 29.18$ %. The average difference per minute is 5.93 % CPU utilization. The relative error of the instance count is $RE_{InstanceCount} = 0.64$ %. The overall difference of the instance minutes amounts to 25 instance minutes. The incurred costs account for 5.985$ for the Eucalyptus run. The simulation costs result in 6.365$, which is $RE_{Costs} = 6.34$ %.

In Figure 20, the median of response times for SingleCore.1 are shown. The first peak in the response times of the conducted run at the beginning is smaller and not as long in the simulation. The peak in hour 8 is smaller in the simulation by about 10 milliseconds. The peak in hour 9 is also smaller in the simulation by about 60 milliseconds. After this peak, the simulated response times approximately follow the response times in the conducted run but they differ by an offset of about 20 milliseconds. An exception is the peak in hour 17. The simulated response times, here, differ by 70 milliseconds.

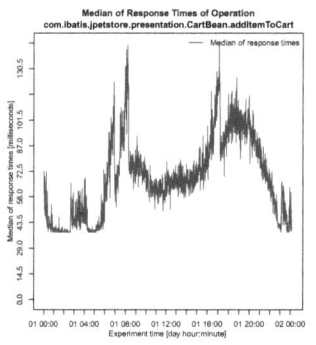 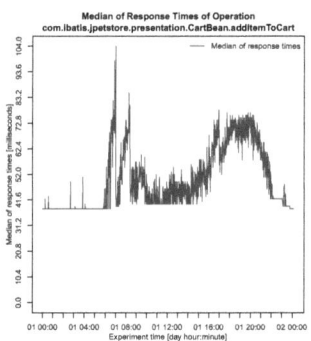

(a) Measured response times (b) Simulated response times (dynamic approach, no S2M)

Figure 20: Median of response times in SingleCore.1 experiment

The relative error for the response times is $RE_{RT} = 24.85$ %. The average difference per minute is 19.03 milliseconds.

The overall relative error for this scenario amounts to $OverallRE = 15.25$ %.

Scenario SingleCore.2

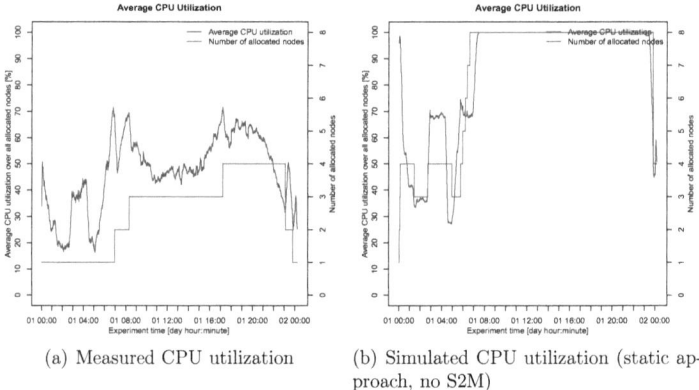

(a) Measured CPU utilization (b) Simulated CPU utilization (static approach, no S2M)

Figure 21: Average CPU utilization of allocated nodes in SingleCore.2 experiment

The CPU utilization and instance count for SingleCore.2 are displayed in Figure 21. At the beginning, the first peak in the simulated CPU utilization is twice as large as the CPU utilization in the conducted run. The instance count in the simulation rises to 4 while the instance count in the conducted run stays at 1. Till hour 6 the CPU utilization is about 25 % larger in the simulation than in the conducted run. The instance count is 1 for the conducted run and ranges between 3 and 4 for the simulation in this time period. In hour 7 the CPU utilization in the simulation increases to 100 % and stays at this utilization till hour 23. In this time frame, the instance count is 8 for the simulation. The CPU utilization of the conducted run ranges from 40 % to 70 % in this period and the instance count is between 2 and 4. At the end, the CPU utilization in the simulation drops to 50 % and the instance count goes down to 4 instances. The conducted run has 20 % CPU utilization and 1 instance in the end.

The relative error for the CPU utilization is $RE_{CPU} = 122.42$ %. The average difference per minute is 38.41 % CPU utilization. The relative error for the instance count amounts to $RE_{InstanceCount} = 203.92$ %. The overall difference of instance minutes is 6,174 instance minutes. Again, the costs for the scenario are 5.985\$. The simulated run costs 16.815\$, which is a relative error of $RE_{Costs} = 180.95$ %.

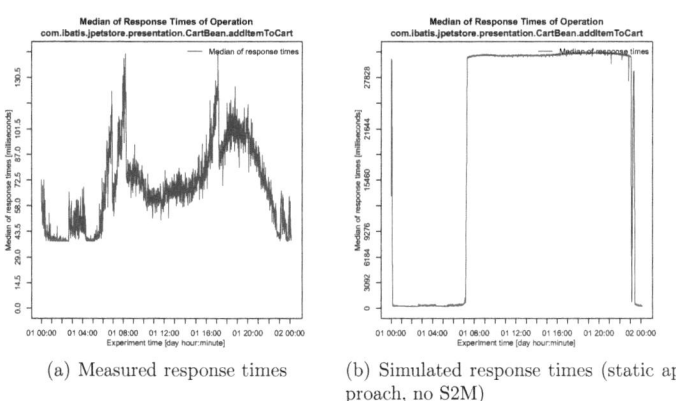

(a) Measured response times

(b) Simulated response times (static approach, no S2M)

Figure 22: Median of response times in SingleCore.2 experiment

Figure 22 displays the median of response times for SingleCore.2. While the response times of the conducted run range between 40 milliseconds and 140 milliseconds, the simulation only has these values between short after the beginning and hour 6, and at the end. At the beginning and between hour 7 and 23 the response times of the simulation are 30 seconds.

$RE_{RT} = 27,597.42$ % is the relative error for the response times and the average difference comes to 20,435.93 milliseconds per minute.

The overall relative error results in $OverallRE = 7,026.17$ %.

Scenario SingleCore.3

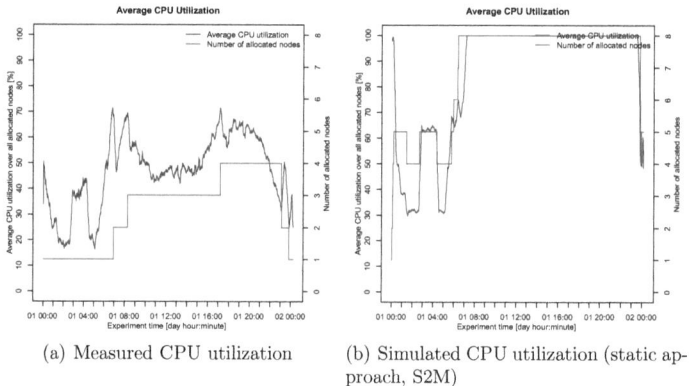

(a) Measured CPU utilization

(b) Simulated CPU utilization (static approach, S2M)

Figure 23: Average CPU utilization of allocated nodes in SingleCore.3 experiment

Figure 23 shows the average CPU utilization of allocated nodes in SingleCore.3 scenario. The run is approximately equal to the scenario SingleCore.2. The difference is that the simulated CPU utilization from hour 1 to 7 is about 30 % higher than the CPU utilization in the conducted run. The instance count is also higher than in the scenario SingleCore.2. It ranges from 4 to 5 in the interval from hour 1 to 7.

The measured values and the simulated values differ by 37.88 % CPU utilization each minute in average. The relative error calculates to $RE_{CPU} = 119.66$ %. The overall difference of instance minutes is 6,528 instance minutes and the relative error is $RE_{InstanceCount} = 228.32$ %. The simulated costs are 17.48\$ and the calculated costs for the Eucalyptus run are 5.985\$. The relative error for the costs is $RE_{Costs} = 192.06$ %.

The median response times for scenario SingleCore.3 are displayed in Figure 24. In the beginning, the response times in the simulation are 30 seconds. After this and to hour 7, they are approximately equal to the response times of the conducted run. From hour 7 to 17, the response times of the simulation range between 60

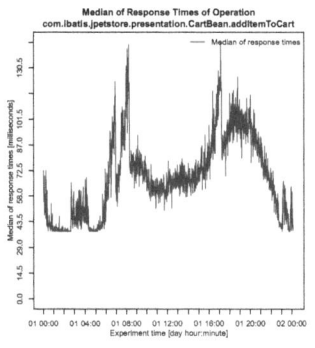
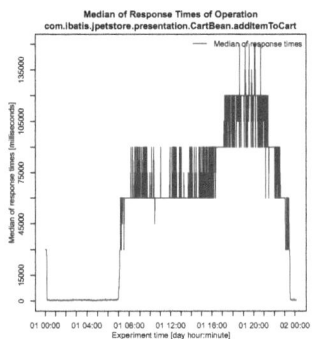

(a) Measured response times

(b) Simulated response times (static approach, S2M)

Figure 24: Median response times in SingleCore.3 experiment

seconds and 90 seconds. Then, from hour 17 to 21 they range from 90 seconds to 150 seconds. Afterwards, they slowly drop to 40 milliseconds.

The relative error is $RE_{RT} = 70,415.88$ %. The average difference between the simulated and measured response times is 53,994.16 milliseconds per minute.

The overall relative error is $OverallRE = 17,738.98$ %.

Scenario SingleCore.4

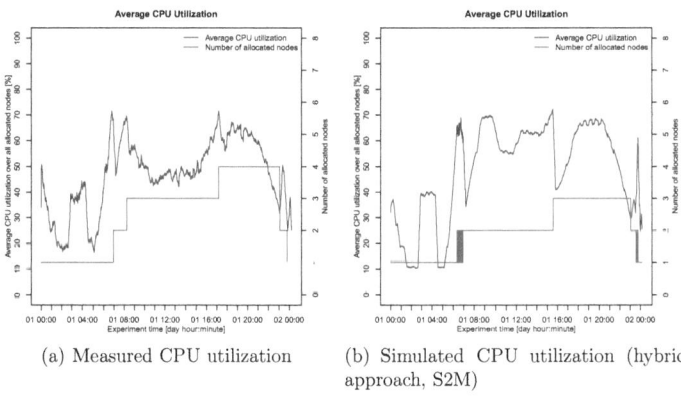

(a) Measured CPU utilization

(b) Simulated CPU utilization (hybrid approach, S2M)

Figure 25: Average CPU utilization of allocated nodes in SingleCore.4 experiment

Figure 25 shows the average CPU utilization of the Eucalyptus run and the simulated values that were produced with the *hybrid approach* and the S2M for SingleCore.4. From the first hour to hour 6, the response times of the simulation and the conducted run are approximately the same. In hour 7, the CPU utilization drops to 40 % in the simulation as opposed to the 50 % CPU utilization of the conducted run. In this hour, the instance count ranges from 1 to 2 which changes every 5 minutes in the simulation and the instance count of the conducted run is 2. In hour 8, the instance count of the conducted run increases to 3. However, the simulated instance count stays at 2. In hour 16, the instance count of the simulation increases to 3. Afterwards, it stays at 3 and decreases to 1 in hour 23. In hour 23, the simulation starts and stops one instance every 5 minutes for half an hour. The instance count of the conducted run increases to 4 in hour 17 and stays till hour 23 where it drops to 1 instance.

The relative error for the CPU utilization is $RE_{CPU} = 41.76$ %. The average difference per minute is 10.65 % CPU utilization. The relative error of the instance count is $RE_{InstanceCount} = 17.79$ %. The overall difference of the instance minutes amounts to 821 instance minutes. The incurred costs account for 5.985$ for the Eucalyptus run. The simulation costs result in 7.03$, which is $RE_{Costs} = 17.46$ %.

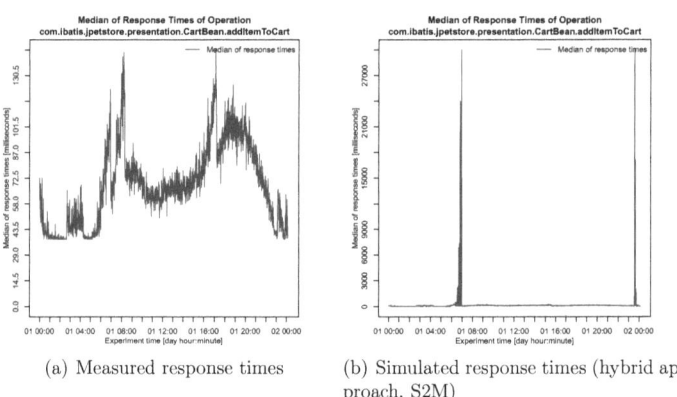

(a) Measured response times

(b) Simulated response times (hybrid approach, S2M)

Figure 26: Median response times in SingleCore.4 experiment

Figure 26 shows the median response times for the scenario SingleCore.4. The response times of the simulation range between 39 milliseconds and 130 milliseconds except in hour 7 and hour 23, the simulated response times are 30 seconds.

$RE_{RT} = 311.57$ % is the relative error for the response times and the average difference comes to 213.81 milliseconds per minute.

The overall relative error results in $OverallRE = 97.14$ %.

Scenario SingleCore.5

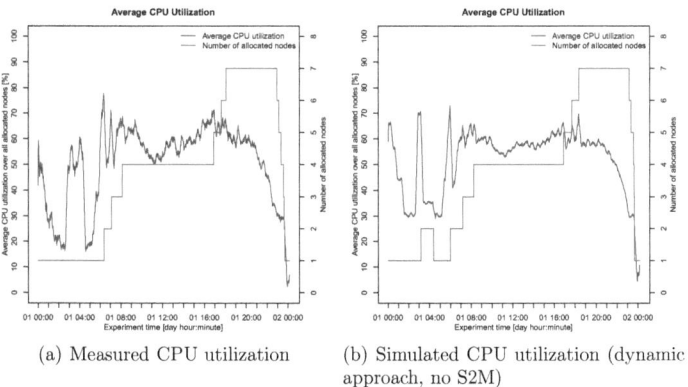

(a) Measured CPU utilization

(b) Simulated CPU utilization (dynamic approach, no S2M)

Figure 27: Average CPU utilization of allocated nodes in SingleCore.5 experiment

Figure 27 displays the average CPU utilization of allocated nodes and the instance count for SingleCore.5 utilizing the *dynamic approach* in no S2M. The peak in the CPU utilization at the beginning is 10 % larger in the simulation than in the conducted run. Afterwards, it drops to 20 % in the conducted run and to 30 % in the simulation. In the simulation, there is a peak at hour 3 with 70 % CPU utilization. The instance count in the simulation increases to 2 in this hour. In contrast, the conducted run reaches 50 to 60 % CPU utilization from hour 3 to 5 and the instance count stays at 1 instance. From hour 4 to 5, the simulation has about 35 % CPU utilization. The instance count in the simulation decreases to 1 in hour 5. The rest of the experiment time the CPU utilization and instance count is approximately equal in the simulation and conducted run.

The relative error for the CPU utilization is $RE_{CPU} = 30.86$ %. The average difference per minute is 9.06 % CPU utilization. The relative error for the instance count amounts to $RE_{InstanceCount} = 7.89$ %. The overall difference of instance minutes is 178 instance minutes. The costs for the scenario are 8.93\$ and the simulated run costs are 9.785\$, which is a relative error of $RE_{Costs} = 9.57$ %.

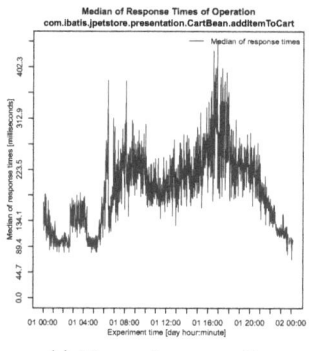 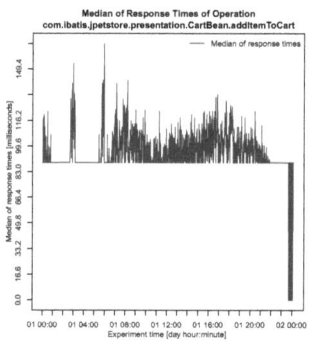

(a) Measured response times   (b) Simulated response times (dynamic approach, no S2M)

Figure 28: Median response times in SingleCore.5 experiment

Figure 28 displays the median of response times for SingleCore.5. At the beginning the response times of the simulation are about 116 milliseconds and the response times of the conducted run are about 160 milliseconds. Then, both drop to 89 milliseconds till hour 3. In hour 3, the simulation shortly peaks to 150 milliseconds and then drops to 89 milliseconds. The response times of the simulated run increase to 160 milliseconds till hour 4 and then drop to 89 milliseconds again. In hour 6, the response times of the simulation peak at 170 milliseconds and the response times of the conducted run peak at 370 milliseconds. The rest of the time the simulated response times follow the response times of the conducted run with an offset of about 100 milliseconds to 200 milliseconds. An exception is made by hour 17, where the response times of the simulated run do not have a high peak with 120 milliseconds but the response times of the conducted run have a peak with 450 milliseconds. Shortly before the end, the simulated response times range from 0 to 89 milliseconds. However, the response times in the conducted run are about 89 milliseconds.

The relative error for the response times is $RE_{RT} = 42.71$ %. The average difference per minute is 91.16 milliseconds.

The overall relative error for this scenario amounts to $OverallRE = 22.75$ %.

Scenario SingleCore.6

The CPU utilization and instance count for SingleCore.6 are displayed in Figure 29. At the beginning, the simulated CPU utilization is about 100 % and drops to 38 %

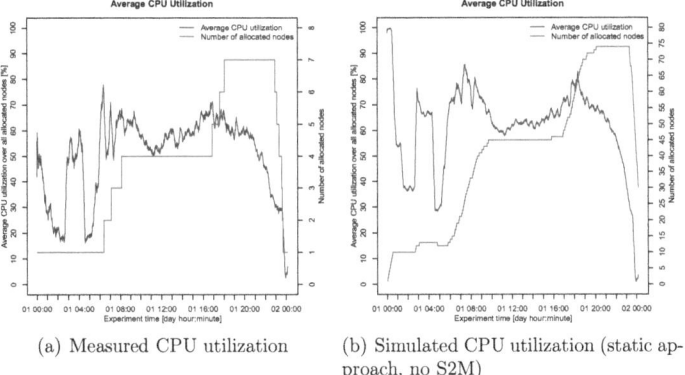

(a) Measured CPU utilization (b) Simulated CPU utilization (static approach, no S2M)

Figure 29: Average CPU utilization of allocated nodes in SingleCore.6 experiment

in hour 1 and the instance count increases to 10 instances. The CPU utilization of the conducted run starts at 60 % and drops to 18 % in hour 2. In hour 3 and 4, the simulated CPU utilization ranges from 65 % to 75 % and the instance count increases to 13. In this period, the CPU utilization of the conducted run ranges between 50 % and 60 % and the instance count is 1 instance. The rest of the experiment time, the CPU utilization of the simulation and the conducted run are approximately the same. However, the instance count is different. From hour 7 to hour 9, the instance count of the simulation increases to 45 instances. In this time period, the instance count of the conducted run increases to 4 instances. From hour 16 to hour 20, the simulated instance count increases to 74 instances and at hour 23 it decreases to 30. The instance count of the conducted run increases from 4 to 7 in hour 17 and hour 18. In hour 23, it drops to 1.

The measured values and the simulated values differ by 12.97 % CPU utilization per minute in average. The relative error calculates to $RE_{CPU} = 39.53$ %. The overall difference of instance minutes is 53,895 instance minutes and the relative error is $RE_{InstanceCount} = 1,059.85$ %. The simulated costs are 103.17\$ and the calculated costs for the Amazon EC2 run are 8.93\$. The relative error for the costs is $RE_{Costs} = 1,055.31$ %.

Figure 30 shows the median response times in SingleCore.6 experiment. In the first hour, the simulated response times are 30 seconds. Afterwards, they range between 90 milliseconds and 1.6 seconds.

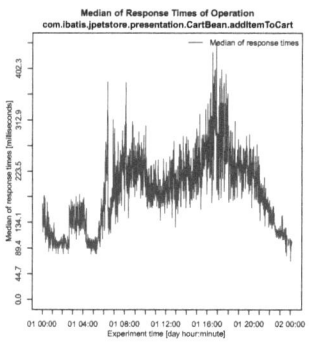 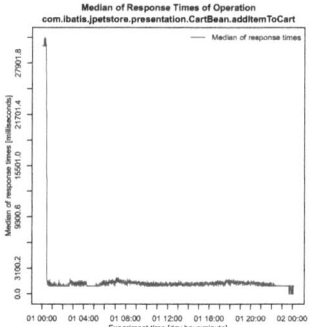

(a) Measured response times

(b) Simulated response times (static approach, no S2M)

Figure 30: Median response times in SingleCore.6 experiment

The relative error is $RE_{RT} = 997.32$ %. The average difference between the simulated and measured response times is 1,551.99 milliseconds per minute.

The overall relative error is $OverallRE = 788.00$ %.

Scenario SingleCore.7

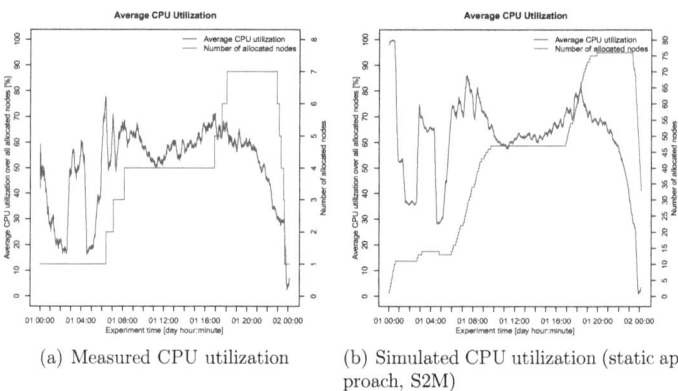

(a) Measured CPU utilization

(b) Simulated CPU utilization (static approach, S2M)

Figure 31: Average CPU utilization of allocated nodes in SingleCore.7 experiment

Figure 31 shows the average CPU utilization of allocated nodes in the SingleCore.7 scenario. The simulated CPU utilization is approximately the same as in in the SingleCore.6 scenario. The only difference is the simulated instance count.

From hour 9 to hour 17, the instance count is 47. The highest instance count is 76 in hour 20 to hour 22.

The relative error for the CPU utilization is $RE_{CPU} = 38.78$ %. The average difference per minute is 12.82 % CPU utilization. The relative error of the instance count is $RE_{InstanceCount} = 1,118.98$ %. The overall difference of the instance minutes amounts to 56,297 instance minutes. The incurred costs account for 8.93\$ for the Amazon EC2 run. The simulation costs result in 107.16\$, which is $RE_{Costs} = 1,100.00$ %.

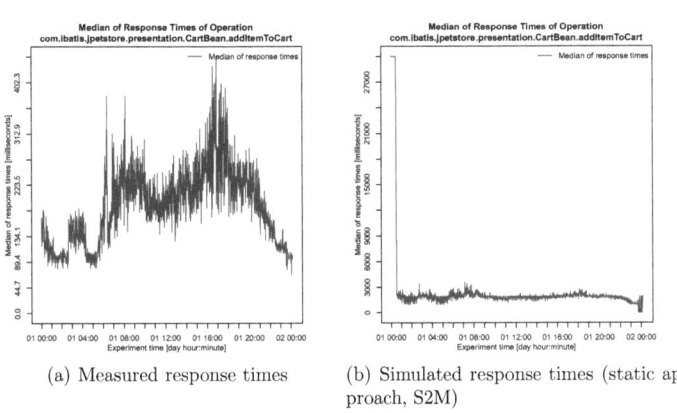

(a) Measured response times (b) Simulated response times (static approach, S2M)

Figure 32: Median response times in SingleCore.7 experiment

The median response times for scenario SingleCore.7 are displayed in Figure 32. The simulated response times are 30 seconds at the beginning. Then, the response times in the simulation range between 90 milliseconds and 3 seconds.

$RE_{RT} = 1,442.79$ % is the relative error for the response times and the average difference comes to 2,272.51 milliseconds per minute.

The overall relative error results in $OverallRE = 925.13$ %.

Scenario SingleCore.8

The CPU utilization and the instance count for SingleCore.8 are displayed in Figure 33. In the first hour, the simulated CPU utilization starts with 95 % and drops to 30 % in hour 2. 4 instances are started and terminated sequentially in the simulation in this time period. The CPU utilization of the conducted run is about 60 % in the first hour and decreases to 18 % until hour 3. The instance count in the conducted run stays at 1 instance. In hour 3, the simulation starts a new instance and

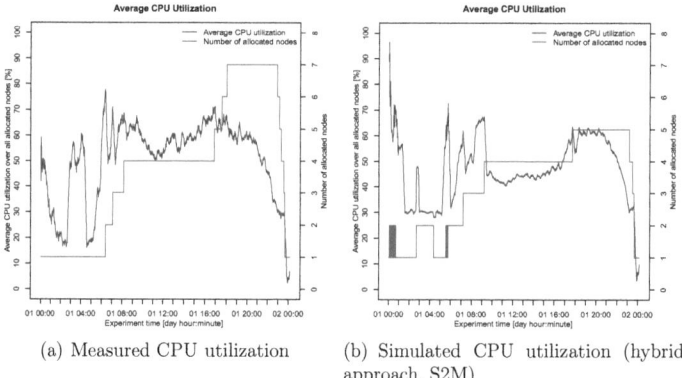

(a) Measured CPU utilization   (b) Simulated CPU utilization (hybrid approach, S2M)

Figure 33: Average CPU utilization of allocated nodes in SingleCore.8 experiment

only peaks at 50 % CPU utilization. Then, the CPU utilization decreases to 30 %. In hour 4, the instance count changes to 1. From hour 3 to 5, the CPU utilization of the conducted run ranges from 48 % to 60 % and the instance count stays 1 instance. At hour 6, the simulated CPU utilization changes to 70 % and 2 new instances are started and 1 instance is terminated sequentially. Then, the CPU utilization drops to 32 %. In hour 7, the instance count of the simulation increases to 3 instances and to 4 instances in hour 9. The instance count in the conducted run changes to 2 instances in hour 6. In hour 7 and hour 8, it changes to 3 instances and then to 4 instances. The simulation increases the instance count to 3 in hour 9. From hour 9 to hour 17, the CPU utilization of the simulation and the conducted run are approximately equal but differ by an offset of 10 % CPU utilization. In hour 17, the simulation increases the instance count to 5 instances. In hour 23, the simulation terminates 4 instances. In hour 17 and 18, the instance count of the conducted run changes from 4 instances to 7 instances. The 7 instances are terminated in hour 23.

The measured values and the simulated values differ by 13.93 % CPU utilization per minute on average. The relative error calculates to $RE_{CPU} = 40.17$ %. The difference of the instance count is 921 instance minutes and the relative error is $RE_{InstanceCount} = 19.66$ %. The simulated costs are 9.405$ and the calculated costs for the Amazon EC2 run are 8.93$. The relative error for the costs is $RE_{Costs} = 5.31$ %.

Figure 34 displays the median of response times for SingleCore.8. At the beginning, the response times in the simulation are 30 seconds. Until hour 1, they are

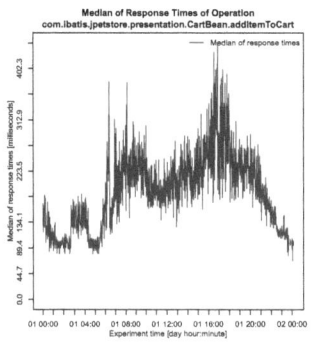 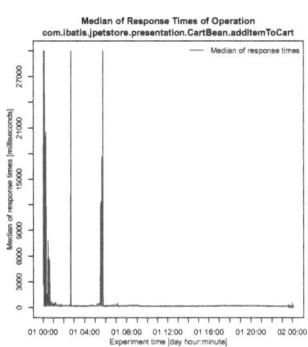

(a) Measured response times (b) Simulated response times (hybrid approach, S2M)

Figure 34: Median response times in SingleCore.8 experiment

decreasing to 500 milliseconds. At hour 3, the simulated response times are 30 seconds for a short duration of 3 minutes. In hour 6, the simulated response times again rise to 30 seconds for 30 minutes. The rest of the experiment time, the response times range between 90 milliseconds and 500 milliseconds in the simulation.

The relative error for the response times is $RE_{RT} = 291.93$ %. The average difference per minute is 396.79 milliseconds.

The overall relative error for this scenario amounts to $OverallRE = 89.26$ %.

8.5.5 Discussion of the Results

This section discusses the results for the scenarios SingleCore.1 to SingleCore.8.

Scenario SingleCore.1

The relative error of the CPU utilization is 29.18 % which is relatively high for the nearly equal looking CPU utilization curve. We attribute this high value to the differences when then CPU utilization is low, i.e. about 16 % in the simulation in contrast to 20 % in the conducted run.

The low instance count relative error shows that the reproduction of the number of used instances of the conducted run is good and is nearly equal to it.

The relative error for the costs is a bit higher than expected from the instance count relative error. The costs for the conducted run and the simulation differ by

4 paid instance hours. These difference probably occurred because the instances at the end were terminated a few minutes too late.

The relative error of about 25 % for the response times is good because we do not simulate initializations of classes. These initializations typically increase the response times when a new virtual machine is started. This is the reason for the third peak to be not visible in the simulated response times.

A value of 15.25 % in the overall relative error is below our threshold of 30 % and hence the simulation provides a sufficiently well reproduction of the conducted run.

Scenario SingleCore.2

In the second scenario, the relative error for the CPU utilization is 122.42 %. This value is too large and does not reproduce the real CPU utilization sufficiently. In most hours, the simulation has twice as large CPU utilization as the conducted run. This fact is founded in the nature of the *static approach*. It typically overestimates the instruction count because it does not consider techniques like JIT. Hence, the workload on the simulated CPU is higher and thus the CPU utilization is larger.

The overestimation of workload on the CPU is also represented in the relative error of the instance count. With 203.92 %, it is large and does not reproduce the conducted run sufficiently. This value would be even larger if our Eucalyptus setup would provide more than 8 instances.

As a consequence of the large difference in the instance count, the relative error for the costs with 180.95 % is also high and not sufficient for reproduction.

The large relative error for the response times of 27,597.42 % results from the timeouts while the CPU utilization is about 100 %.

The overall error amounts to 7,026.17 % which is far beyond our 30 % threshold and hence the *static approach* does not reproduce the conducted run sufficiently.

Scenario SingleCore.3

The results are equally high as in the SingleCore.2 scenario. The relative error for the response times is about 3 times larger than the one of SingleCore.2 because the S2M resulted in more timeouts. The runtime of the entry method increased because most of its submethods timed out.

Given that the overall relative error is 17,738.98 %, the *static approach* in S2M does not reproduce the conducted run sufficiently.

Scenario SingleCore.4

The value 41.76 % for the relative error for CPU utilization is high. We attribute this circumstance to not starting the third instance in hour 8 in the simulation, which resulted from a CPU utilization just slightly under 70 %.

Due to not starting a fourth instance, the relative error for the instance count is 17.79 %.

The relative error for the costs is 17.46 %. For not starting a fourth instance, one would expect that the costs are lower in the simulation. However, the starting and terminating of instances in hour 6 and hour 23 resulted in increased costs. This circumstance could be fixed by an adaptation strategy that is aware of the underlying cost model.

The high value for the relative error of the response times results from the timeout of calls in hour 6 and hour 23 where the simulation started and terminated instances.

The overall relative error for this scenario is 97.14 %. This is over our threshold and hence it does not reproduce the conducted run sufficiently. However, it can be optimized by an adaption strategy that is aware of the cost model.

Scenario SingleCore.5

The relative error of 30.86 % for the CPU utilization mainly results from the time interval between the beginning and hour 7. Here, the CPU utilization in the simulation is larger than in the conducted run. Furthermore, the second instance, which is only started in the simulation, reduces the overall CPU utilization.

The second instance from hour 3 to 5 also caused the relative error for the instance count and the costs to be higher than what could have been expected of the nearly equal looking instance count.

At the high relative error for the response times we can see that the response times do not sufficiently reproduce the response times of the conducted run. From hour 7 to hour 22 the response times in the conducted run are about twice as large as the simulation. We attribute this circumstance to the potentially large range of MIPIPS on *m1.small* instances in the Amazon EC2 run. Like E1 has shown, the newly started instances might have a lower MIPIPS value than the first *m1.small* instance which results in higher response times.

Since the overall relative error is 22.75 %, the scenario reproduces the conducted run sufficiently.

Scenario SingleCore.6

39.53 % is the relative error for the CPU utilization which is mainly the consequence of the time interval between the beginning and hour 9. In this time period, the CPU utilization of the simulation is twice as large as the CPU utilization in the conducted run. Again, the *static approach* mostly overestimates the instruction count of the methods. Hence, the simulated CPU utilization was higher than in the conducted run.

The large difference from maximal 75 instances in the simulation to 7 instances in the conducted run results in a high relative error of 1,059.85 % for the instance count and a high relative error of 1,055.31 % for the costs.

The relative error for the response times is also high with 997.32 %. Most of the time, the simulated CPU utilization was higher than the one in the conducted run. In this case, this results in higher response times. Furthermore, the CPU utilization of about 100 % in the beginning in the simulation resulted in timeouts of service calls.

The overall relative error amounts to 788 % which is larger than 30 % and thus the *static approach* without separate submethod calls does not reproduce the conducted run sufficiently in Amazon EC2.

Scenario SingleCore.7

The relative error for the CPU utilization is approximately equal to SingleCore.6. However, the relative error for the instance count and costs are about 60 % higher than in SingleCore.6. The simulation with separate submethods is not accurate which submethod should be called due to if-statements. Thus, the instance count was higher with 2 additional instances.

The response times' relative error of 1,442.78 % is about 450 % larger than in SingleCore.6. We attribute this circumstance to the former described larger workload on the nodes. In addition, scheduling effects might have influenced the response times because there are more Cloudlets to be processed in the S2M.

The overall relative error is 925.13 %. This is over our threshold of 30 % and hence the scenario does not reproduce the conducted run sufficiently.

Scenario SingleCore.8

The relative error for the CPU utilization is 40.17 %. This mainly results because at the beginning until hour 8 the simulation differs from the conducted run which is the result of starting new instances at the beginning and in hour 3.

The value for the relative error of instance count is 19.66 % which results from the starting of new instances in the beginning and in hour 3 in the simulation. Furthermore, the simulation does not start 2 instances in hour 17 which is done by the conducted run.

The relative error for the costs amounts 5.31 %. The instances started at the beginning add to the costs. From hour 17 to hour 23, the simulation has only 5 started instances in contrast to 7 instances in the conducted run. This reduces the costs. Hence, the relative error for the costs is low because the former described circumstances result in a small difference of the costs.

The high value for the relative error of 291.93 % for the response times results from the timeouts that are created by the starting and terminating instances in a small time period in the beginning, in hour 3, and hour 6.

89.26 % is the overall relative error. It lies above our threshold of 30 % and thus is too high to reproduce the conducted run sufficiently. However, like in the scenario SingleCore.4 this can be improved by using a cost model aware adaptation strategy.

8.5.6 Threats to Validity

For Amazon EC2, the threats we described under E1 also hold for this evaluation.

An evaluation with one program is not necessarily generalizable. With JPetStore, our simulation performs well at least with the *dynamic approach*. However, with other applications this is not necessarily the fact and should be further researched.

8.6 E3: Accuracy Evaluation for Multi Core Instances

This section describes the accuracy evaluation for the simulation of multi core instances.

8.6.1 Goals

This evaluation has the same goal as E2. Though, it evaluates the accuracy validity of CDOSim for multi core instances.

8.6.2 Experimental Setting

The experiment setup was described in Section 8.3. For the Eucalyptus run, we use the instance type *m1.xlarge* and the maximal arrival rate amounts to 6,709 calls per minute. On Eucalyptus, *m1.xlarge* has two cores. For the Amazon EC2 run, we use the instance type *c1.medium*. Here, the maximal arrival rate is 6,472 calls per minute and *c1.medium* also has two cores. Both runs start with one instance, which will not be terminated.

8.6.3 Scenarios

The evaluation includes two scenarios.

Scenario MultiCore.1: Simulate with dynamic approach in no S2M for Eucalyptus run with m1.xlarge

The simulation takes place on the basis of a workload from a run that was conducted on Eucalyptus with *m1.xlarge*. The simulation is configured to use the *dynamic approach* and to not simulate separate submethod calls.

Scenario MultiCore.2: Simulate with dynamic approach in no S2M for Amazon EC2 run with c1.medium

The simulation takes place on the basis of a workload from a run that was conducted on Amazon EC2 with *c1.medium*. The approach for instruction counting is the *dynamic approach* and the simulation does not model separate submethod calls.

8.6.4 Results

In this sections the results for E3 are shown.

Scenario MultiCore.1

The CPU utilization and instance count for MultiCore.1 are displayed in Figure 35. The CPU utilization and instance count in the simulation approximately equal the CPU utilization and instance count of the conducted run.

The relative error for the CPU utilization is $RE_{CPU} = 26.53$ %. The average difference per minute is 5.44 % CPU utilization. The relative error of the instance count is $RE_{InstanceCount} = 1.37$ %. The overall difference of the instance minutes amounts to 39 instance minutes. The incurred costs account for 6.84\$ for the Eucalyptus run. The simulation costs result in 7.22\$, which is $RE_{Costs} = 5.55$ %.

In Figure 36 the median of response times for MultiCore.1 are shown. From the beginning until hour 8, the simulation and the conducted run have the response times 38 milliseconds. The first peak in hour 8 is smaller in the simulation by a difference of about 22 milliseconds. From hour 12 to hour 15, the simulated response times range

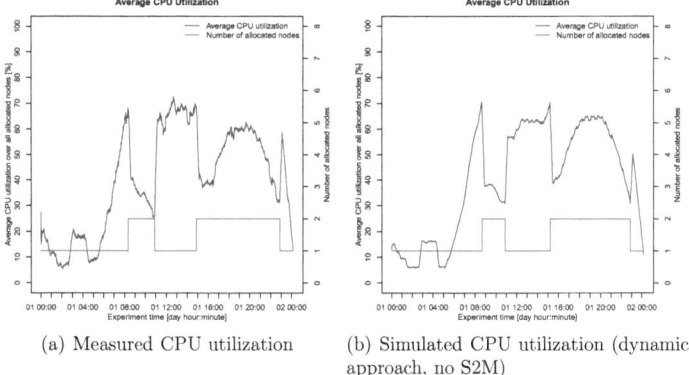

(a) Measured CPU utilization   (b) Simulated CPU utilization (dynamic approach, no S2M)

Figure 35: Average CPU utilization of allocated nodes in MultiCore.1 experiment

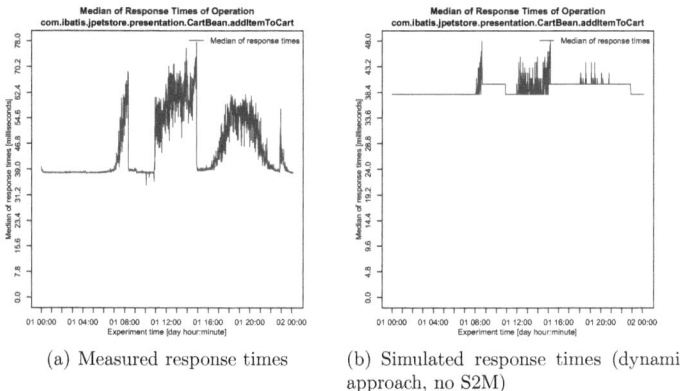

(a) Measured response times   (b) Simulated response times (dynamic approach, no S2M)

Figure 36: Median response times in MultiCore.1 experiment

from 38 to 48 milliseconds. The conducted run's response times range from 38 to 78 milliseconds in this time interval. The rest of the experiment time, the response times of the simulation are between 38 milliseconds and 43 milliseconds. In this time period, the conducted run has response times between 38 and 60 milliseconds.

The relative error is $RE_{RT} = 12.41$ %. The average difference between the simulated and measured response times is 6.90 milliseconds per minute.

The overall relative error is $OverallRE = 11.46$ %.

Scenario MultiCore.2

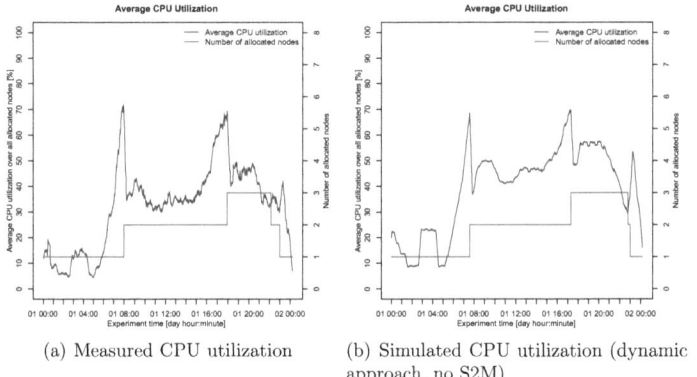

(a) Measured CPU utilization

(b) Simulated CPU utilization (dynamic approach, no S2M)

Figure 37: Average CPU utilization of allocated nodes in MultiCore.2 experiment

The CPU utilization and instance count for MultiCore.2 are displayed in Figure 37. The instance count of the simulation approximately equals the instance count of the conducted run. The only difference occurs in hour 22. Here, the conducted run terminates the third instance. In contrast, the simulation terminates the third instance in the hour 23. The CPU utilization curve is also approximately the same in the simulation and the conducted run. However, most of the time they differ by an offset of 10 % CPU utilization.

The relative error for the CPU utilization is $RE_{CPU} = 46.86$ %. The average difference per minute is 9.87 % CPU utilization. The relative error for instance count amounts to $RE_{InstanceCount} = 4.37$ %. The overall difference of instance minutes is 102 instance minutes. Again, the costs for the scenario are 5.32$. The simulated run costs 5.70$, which is a relative error of $RE_{Costs} = 7.14$ %.

In Figure 38 the median of response times for MultiCore.2 are shown. The first peak in hour 8 and the second peak in hour 17 is contained in the simulation and the conducted run. However, the first peak is 109 milliseconds in the conducted run and 62 milliseconds in the simulation. The second peak is 120 milliseconds in the conducted run and 50 milliseconds in the simulation. The rest of the experiment time, the simulated response times stay at 49 milliseconds while the response times of the conducted run range between 49 milliseconds and 74 milliseconds.

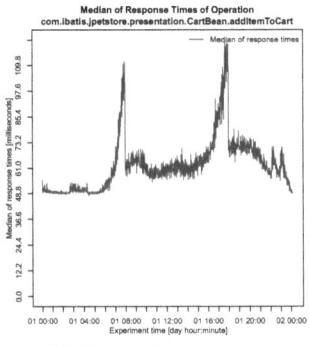
(a) Measured response times

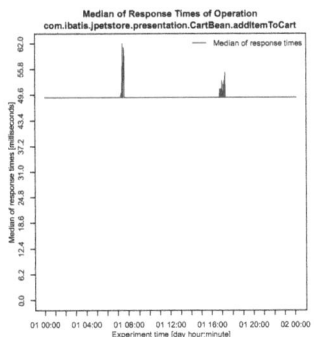
(b) Simulated response times (dynamic approach, no S2M)

Figure 38: Median response times in MultiCore.2 experiment

The relative error is $RE_{RT} = 18.79$ %. The average difference between the simulated and measured response times is 13.32 milliseconds per minute.

The overall relative error is $OverallRE = 19.29$ %.

8.6.5 Discussion of the Results

This section discusses the results for E3.

Scenario MultiCore.1

The relative error for the CPU utilization is 26.53 % which is below our 30 % threshold and thus the simulation sufficiently reproduces the CPU utilization of the conducted run.

The low relative error of 1.37 % for the instance count shows that the reproduction of the number of used instances of the conducted run is good and is nearly equal to it.

The relative error for the costs of 5.55 % is a bit higher than expected from the low instance count relative error. This results from the increased price for a multi core instance.

The relative error of about 12.41 % for the response times is the lowest of all experiments and below our threshold. Thus, the response times are also sufficiently well reproduced.

The overall relative error of 11.46 % is below our 30 % threshold and thus the simulation sufficiently reproduces the conducted run.

Scenario MultiCore.2

The relative error for the CPU utilization is 46.86 % which is a rather high value. We attribute this circumstance to the constant offset of about 10 % CPU utilization most of the time which might have occurred from a too low MIPIPS value.

In accordance to the low relative error of the instance count, the relative error for the costs is also low.

The relative error for the response times is 18.79 % which is below our threshold.

A value of 19.29 % in the overall relative error is below our threshold of 30 % and hence the simulation provides a sufficiently well reproduction of the conducted run.

8.6.6 Threats to Validity

All described threats for validity in E2 are applicable in this evaluation. In addition, we only conducted runs with *m1.xlarge* on Eucalyptus and *c1.medium* on Amazon EC2 and thus the results might be different if we would use other multi core instances.

8.7 E4: Accuracy Evaluation for Adaptation Strategy Configurations

In this section the evaluation for adaption strategy configurations is described.

8.7.1 Goals

E2 and E3 used 70 % and 30 % CPU utilization thresholds for adaptation of nodes. This evaluation shows that the simulation reproduces a conducted run with other adaptation strategies sufficiently.

8.7.2 Experimental Setting

The experiment setup was described in Section 8.3. For the Eucalyptus run, we use the instance type *m1.small* and the maximal arrival rate amounts 5,564 calls per minute. For the Amazon EC2 run, we use the instance type *m1.small*. Here, the maximal arrival rate is 3,832 calls per minute. The adaptation strategy is 90 % CPU utilization for starting a new instance and 10 % CPU utilization for terminating a running instance. Both runs start with one instance, which will not be terminated.

8.7.3 Scenarios

Two scenarios are part of this evaluation.

Scenario Adaptation.1: Simulate with dynamic approach in no S2M for Eucalyptus run with 90 % and 10 % CPU utilization adaptation strategy

The workload is recorded with *m1.small* instances on Eucalyptus with a 90 % and 10 % CPU utilization adaptation strategy. The simulation uses the *dynamic approach* and does not simulate separate submethod calls.

Scenario Adaptation.2: Simulate with dynamic approach in no S2M for Amazon EC2 run with 90 % and 10 % CPU utilization adaptation strategy

This is the same scenario like Adaptation.1 except that the workload is recorded with *m1.small* instances on Amazon EC2.

8.7.4 Results

The results for E4 are described in the following.

Scenario Adaptation.1

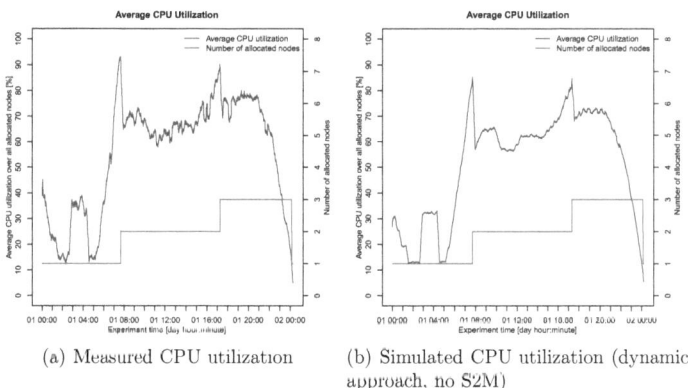

(a) Measured CPU utilization

(b) Simulated CPU utilization (dynamic approach, no S2M)

Figure 39: Average CPU utilization of allocated nodes in Adaptation.1 experiment

The CPU utilization and the instance count for Adaptation.1 are displayed in Figure 39. Both are approximately equal in the simulation and conducted run.

105

The measured values and the simulated values differ by 6.56 % CPU utilization per minute on average. The relative error calculates to $RE_{CPU} = 17.66$ %. The difference regarding the instance count is 8 instance minutes and the relative error is $RE_{InstanceCount} = 0.24$ %. The simulated costs are 4.845\$ and the calculated costs for the Eucalyptus run are 4.655\$. The relative error for the costs is $RE_{Costs} = 4.08$ %.

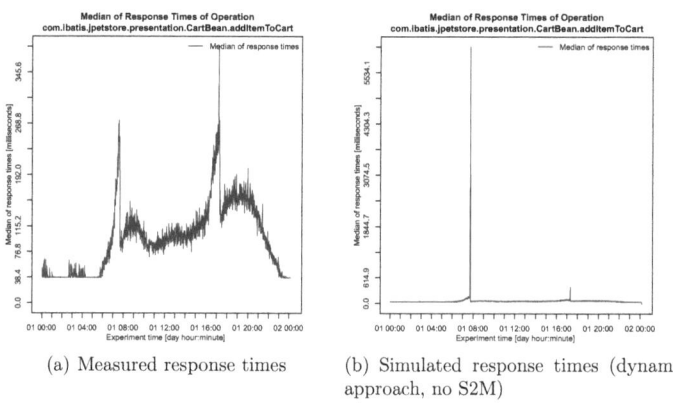

(a) Measured response times

(b) Simulated response times (dynamic approach, no S2M)

Figure 40: Median response times in Adaptation.1 experiment

Figure 40 shows the median response times for scenario Adaptation.1. The two peaks of the response times in the conducted run are also included in the simulation. However, the first peak in the simulation is at 6,149 milliseconds. In the conducted run, the first peak is at 268 milliseconds. The second peak is at 315 milliseconds in the simulation and at 383 milliseconds in the conducted run. The rest of the experiment time, the response times of the conducted run range between 38 milliseconds and 192 milliseconds and the simulated response times range between 38 milliseconds and 300 milliseconds.

The relative error is $RE_{RT} = 40.06$ %. The average difference between the simulated and measured response times is 46.59 milliseconds per minute.

The overall relative error is $OverallRE = 15.51$ %.

Scenario Adaptation.2

Figure 41 shows the average CPU utilization of the allocated nodes in the Adaptation.2 scenario. The instance count in the simulation and the conducted run is approximately equal. The CPU utilization is also roughly equal except from the

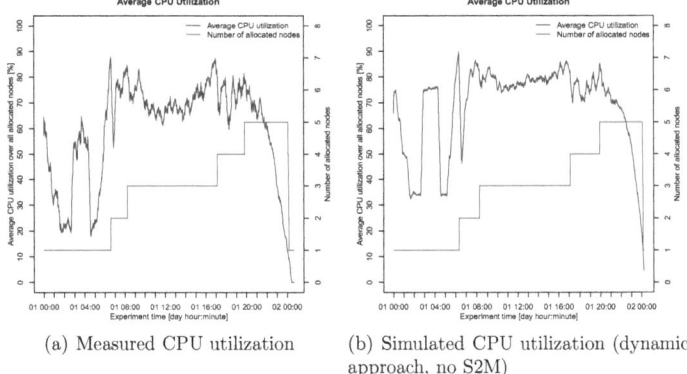

(a) Measured CPU utilization (b) Simulated CPU utilization (dynamic approach, no S2M)

Figure 41: Average CPU utilization of allocated nodes in Adaptation.2 experiment

beginning to hour 6. In this time period, the simulated CPU utilization differs by an offset of about 10 % CPU utilization.

The relative error for the CPU utilization is $RE_{CPU} = 30.64$ %. The average difference per minute is 12.04 % CPU utilization. The relative error of the instance count is $RE_{InstanceCount} = 1.32$ %. The overall difference of the instance minutes amounts to 28 instance minutes. The incurred costs account for 6.745\$ for the Amazon EC2 run. The simulation costs result in 7.125\$, which is $RE_{Costs} = 5.63$ %.

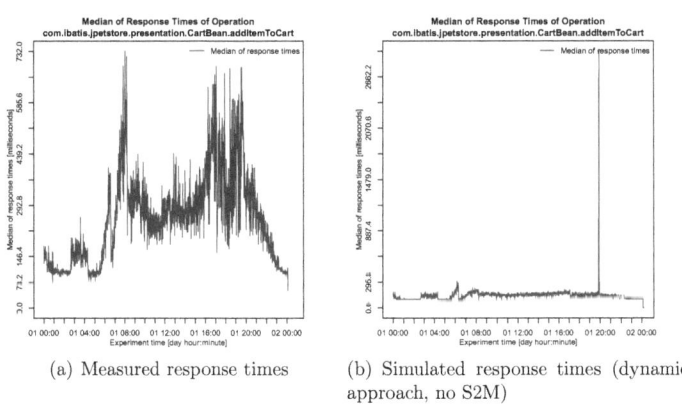

(a) Measured response times (b) Simulated response times (dynamic approach, no S2M)

Figure 42: Median response times in Adaptation.2 experiment

107

The median response times for scenario Adaptation.2 are displayed in Figure 42. In hour 6, there is a peak in the simulated response times with 295 milliseconds and in the response times this peak is 390 milliseconds. The high peak of response times in the conducted run in hour 7 does not show up as a peak in the simulated response times. In hour 20, the simulation has a peak in the response times with 2,903 milliseconds. The rest of the experiment time, the simulated response times range from 80 milliseconds to 210 milliseconds and the response times in the conducted run range from 80 milliseconds to 439 milliseconds.

The relative error for the response times is $RE_{RT} = 37.57$ %. The average difference per minute is 120.29 milliseconds.

The overall relative error for this scenario amounts to $OverallRE = 18.79$ %.

8.7.5 Discussion of the Results

In this section the results for E4 are discussed.

Scenario Adaptation.1

17.66 % is the relative error for the CPU utilization which is rather low in comparison to the other evaluations. Furthermore, it is under our threshold of 30 % and thus sufficiently accurate.

The low relative error of 0.24 % for the instance count and the low relative error of 4.08 % for the costs show that the reproduction is sufficient well in respect to these attributes and also nearly equal to the conducted run.

The relative error for the response times is 40.06 %. We attribute this rather high value to the high simulated response times in hour 8.

Since the overall relative error is 15.51 %, the scenario reproduces the conducted run sufficiently.

Scenario Adaptation.2

The relative error for the CPU utilization is 30.64 % which we attribute mainly to the differences from hour 1 to hour 6.

The relative error of 1.32 % for the instance count shows that the reproduction of the number of used instances of the conducted run is sufficiently good.

The relative error of 5.63 % for the costs is also low and shows that the reproduction is sufficiently accurate.

The relative error for the response times is 37.57 %. We attribute this rather high value to the high response times that were simulated in hour 20.

The overall relative error of 18.79 % is below our 30 % threshold and thus the simulation sufficiently reproduces the conducted run.

8.7.6 Threats to Validity

All described threats for validity from E2 also are applicable in this evaluation. Furthermore, only one adaptation strategy was tested. Thus, it is not generalizable but shows that the 90 % and 10 % CPU utilization adaptation strategy provides good results.

8.8 E5: Inter-Cloud Accuracy Evaluation

In this section the evaluation for inter-cloud accuracy is described.

8.8.1 Goals

This evaluation has the goal of predicting the run for a cloud provider platform, for example Eucalyptus, on the basis of a run, that was conducted with a different cloud provider platform, for example Amazon EC2.

8.8.2 Experimental Setting

The experiment setup was described in Section 8.3. First, a run on Amazon EC2 with *c1.medium* instances is conducted. The workload intensity is 6,472 calls per minute at the maximum. For the Eucalyptus run, we use the instance type *m1.small* and the maximal arrival rate amounts 6,402 calls per minute.

8.8.3 Scenario

The evaluation includes one scenario.

Scenario PredictionAmazon.1: Simulate with dynamic approach in no S2M an Eucalyptus run from a real Amazon EC2 run

The workload is recorded with *c1.medium* instances on Amazon EC2. Then, the simulation predicts on the basis of this workload the CPU utilization, instance count, costs, and response times for the case that the run would be conducted with Eucalyptus and *m1.small* instances. Afterwards, a run with the same workload intensity is carried out on Eucalyptus. The simulation uses the *dynamic approach* and does not simulate separate submethod calls.

8.8.4 Results

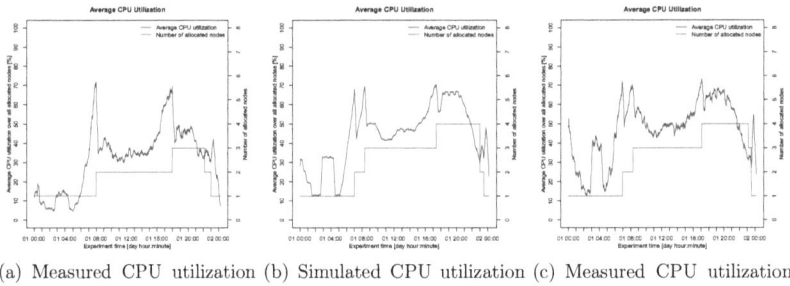

(a) Measured CPU utilization in Amazon EC2 run (b) Simulated CPU utilization (dynamic approach, no S2M) (c) Measured CPU utilization in Eucalyptus run

Figure 43: Average CPU utilization of allocated nodes in PredictionAmazon.1 experiment

The CPU utilization and instance count for PredictionAmazon.1 are displayed in Figure 43. The left subfigure shows the conducted run on Amazon EC2. We describe the predicted CPU utilization in comparison to the afterwards conducted run on Eucalyptus. The CPU utilization of the predicted run and the Eucalyptus run are approximately the same. However, they differ at the beginning and from hour 3 to hour 5. At the beginning, the simulated CPU utilization is 30 % but the conducted run has 52 %. From hour 3 to 5, the CPU utilization of the simulation is 32 % while the conducted run has about 40 % in this interval. The instance count is also approximately the same for both except in hour 23 where the Eucalyptus run terminates the third instance 10 minutes later than the simulation.

The relative error for the CPU utilization is $RE_{CPU} = 21.60$ %. The average difference per minute is 6.53 % CPU utilization. The relative error of the instance count is $RE_{InstanceCount} = 1.32$ %. The overall difference of the instance minutes amounts to 62 instance minutes. The incurred costs account for 6.175$ for the Eucalyptus run. The simulation costs result in 6.27$, which is $RE_{Costs} = 1.53$ %.

In Figure 44 the median of response times for PredictionAmazon.1 are shown. The first two small peaks in the first hour and hour 4 are not contained in the sim-

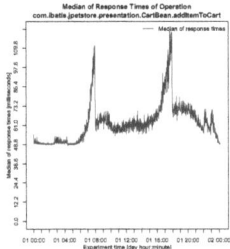 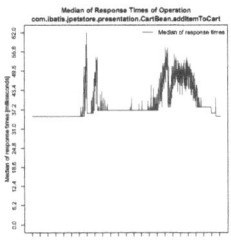 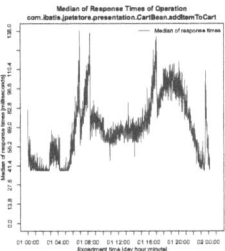

(a) Measured response times in Amazon EC2 run (b) Simulated response times (dynamic approach, no S2M) (c) Measured response times in Eucalyptus run

Figure 44: Median response times in PredictionAmazon.1 experiment

ulation. The third and fourth peak in hour 7 and 8 are contained in the simulation. However, they differ by about 76 milliseconds from the ones in the conducted run. The fifth peak at hour 19 is again contained in the simulation but is 83 milliseconds lower. The following hill is about 65 milliseconds lower than in the conducted run.

$RE_{RT} = 38.62$ % is the relative error for the response times and the average difference comes to 29.51 milliseconds per minute.

The overall relative error results in $OverallRE = 15.76$ %.

8.8.5 Discussion of the Results

The relative error for the CPU utilization is 21.60 % and thus the simulation sufficiently well predicts the CPU utilization.

The relative error of 1.32 % for the instance count shows that the prediction of the number of used instances of the Eucalyptus run is good and is nearly equal to it. The same applies for the relative error of 1.53 % for the costs.

38.62 % is the relative error for the response times. This value is rather high in comparison to the other low relative errors. We attribute this circumstance mainly to not modeling the initialization time of Java classes.

The overall relative error of 15.76 % is below our 30 % threshold and thus the simulation sufficiently predicts the run using Eucalyptus.

8.8.6 Threats to Validity

The threats to validity from E2 also are applicable in this evaluation. Furthermore, we only conducted a prediction from a run with *c1.medium* instances on

Amazon EC2 to *m1.small* instances on Eucalyptus. The simulation might not yield good results if we conduct predictions for other instance types or cloud providers.

8.9 Summary

E2, E3, and E4 evaluated the replicative validity of our simulation. They showed that the *dynamic approach* without S2M provides sufficiently good results for single core instances, multi core instances, and other adaptation strategies. The *static approach* produced insufficient results. The *hybrid approach* proved insufficient with our threshold of 30 %. However, it can be further enhanced with a cost model aware adaptation strategy. This is an important improvement to make because the *hybrid approach* is the only applicable approach for S2M. This results from the fact that the *dynamic approach* in most cases does not have its preconditions satisfied, i.e., not all methods have associated response times from dynamic analysis, and the *static approach* produces insufficient results that differ by a large factor from the conducted runs.

E5 addressed the predictive and structural validity. It showed that the inter-cloud prediction is possible and provides sufficient predictive accuracy. The structural validity is also fulfilled because the simulated prediction follows approximately the CPU utilization of the conducted run, although the CPU utilization was recorded with a multi core instance and MIPIPS are per core. Hence, the simulation follows the structure of real runs.

Therefore, all three validities are fulfilled and thus the simulation model is valid and provides useful results.

Table 14 shows an overview of the relative errors for each scenario. The relative errors were already discussed in the corresponding evaluation.

Scenario	RE_{CPU}	$RE_{InstanceCount}$	RE_{Costs}	RE_{RT}	$OverallRE$
SingleCore.1	29.18 %	0.64 %	6.34 %	24.85 %	15.25 %
SingleCore.2	122.42 %	203.92 %	180.95 %	27,597.42 %	7,026.17 %
SingleCore.3	119.66 %	228.32 %	192.06 %	70,415.88 %	17,738.98 %
SingleCore.4	41.76 %	17.79 %	17.46 %	311.57 %	97.14 %
SingleCore.5	30.86 %	7.89 %	9.57 %	42.71 %	22.75 %
SingleCore.6	39.53 %	1,059.85 %	1,055.31 %	997.32 %	788.00 %
SingleCore.7	38.78 %	1,118.98 %	1,100.00 %	1,442.79 %	925.13 %
SingleCore.8	40.17 %	19.66 %	5.31 %	291.93 %	89.26 %
MultiCore.1	26.53 %	1.37 %	5.55 %	12.41 %	11.46 %
MultiCore.2	46.86 %	4.37 %	7.14 %	18.79 %	19.29 %
Adaptation.1	17.66 %	0.24 %	4.08 %	40.06 %	15.51 %
Adaptation.2	30.64 %	1.32 %	5.63 %	37.57 %	18.79 %
Prediction.1	21.60 %	1.32 %	1.53 %	38.62 %	15.76 %

Table 14: Overview of the relative error values for each scenario

9 Related Work

This section lists and describes the related work that ranges from other simulators (Sections 9.1 to 9.4), over another instruction counting method (Section 9.5), over another output metric (Section 9.6), to other benchmarks (Sections 9.7 and 9.8).

9.1 GroudSim

Like CloudSim, GroudSim is a tool for simulating clouds environments. It is developed by Ostermann et al. [52]. In contrast to CloudSim, GroudSim also provides support for the simulation of Grids. Furthermore, GroudSim utilizes an event-based simulator that requires only one thread per simulation, while CloudSim follows a process-based approach that runs a separate thread for each entity. The equivalent to Cloudlets in CloudSim are GroudJobs in GroudSim. A further feature of GroudSim is the definition of failures. Failures can be generated in a defined interval for a specific registered resource.

For us, GroudSim was no alternative to CloudSim because we did not discover an official release of GroudSim on the web. GroudSim is only available as an SVN version and seems to be not under active development due to the last conducted commit in the year 2010.

9.2 Palladio

Palladio [3] was started in 2003 at the University of Oldenburg and is a well-validated, tool-supported software architecture simulation approach. Its main objective is the prediction of Quality of Service (QoS) properties of component-based software architectures. Thus, helping to create a high quality software architecture with dependable quality properties. The tool support is named Palladio Bench. It is integrated into Eclipse and enables the usage of R. Palladio supports four quality dimensions. These are performance, reliability, maintenance, and costs. A central role in Palladio has the Palladio Component Model (PCM) which models different aspects of a component.

9.3 SLAstic.SIM

SLAstic.SIM [72] is a performance simulator for runtime configurable component-based software systems utilizing SLAstic. The online-adaptation framework SLAstic was already described in Section 8.3.1. The system, that should be simulated, must be modeled as an instance of the PCM for SLAstic.SIM. Furthermore, SLAstic.SIM requires external workload traces and reconfiguration plans for simulation. SLAstic.SIM helps to predict the performance impact of specific reconfiguration actions and thus it can support the evaluation of different adaptation strategies.

Our CDOSim software has similarities to SLAstic.SIM in some aspects. SLAstic.SIM's main objective is to find the best performance in respect to response times. CDOSim has the main objective to find the best trade off between high performance and low costs. Furthermore, SLAstic.SIM differs in the preconditions for the simulation. It requires to have a PCM instance available that is typically built with the support of system specialists. In contrast to SLAstic.SIM, CDOSim requires the availability of the source code represented as a KDM instance. KDM instances of the source code can be generated automatically and thus CDOSim requires less human effort. SLAstic.SIM and CDOSim can simulate and evaluate different adaptation strategies. Though, this aspect is only one part of a cloud deployment option. CDOSim can also simulate the other parts of a cloud deployment option which are only partly supported by SLAstic.SIM.

9.4 iCanCloud

iCanCloud [47, 48] is a simulation platform for modeling and simulating existing and non-existing cloud computing architectures. It is mainly aimed for the prediction of the trade off between costs and performance of a specific application in a specific cloud environment and configuration. Furthermore, it bases on the SIMCAN simulation framework [49]. In iCanCloud, the user can model applications using traces of real applications, using state graphs, and programming new applications directly in the simulation platform. However, it does not provide support for importing existing software systems easily. These must be modeled manually.

9.5 Byte Instruction Count for Java

The Java Resource Accounting Framework 2 (J-RAF2) [26], that's first version was originally developed by Yaksiè [76], provides a portable bytecode instruction counting scheme for Java applications. J-RAF2 instruments the bytecode instructions of Java classes which makes the executed instructions explicit. At runtime, each thread maintains its own bytecode instruction count, which is afterwards summed up with the ones of other threads for an overall bytecode instruction count. A special feature of J-RAF2 is that it also instruments JDK methods. Camesi et al. [11] discovered that there exists a stable, application-specific ratio of bytecodes per unit of CPU time on the platforms that were tested by them.

Another approach for byte instruction counting in Java is ByCounter by Kuperberg [39, 40]. This approach is aimed at being light-weight. It only instruments the application bytecode and not the JVM. Hence, it can be used on every available JVM.

We assume that byte instruction counting for Java applications can improve our approaches for instruction counting. However, it is only applicable for Java and not for other programming languages. Hence, we first developed language independent instruction counting approaches. Applying language specific instruction counting methods might optimize the precision of the simulation.

9.6 Measuring Elasticity

Elasticity is an additional metric that CDOSim could produce as an output. Islam et al. [30] propose a method for measuring the elasticity of an application on a specific cloud provider which is motivated by a paper of Weinman [75]. They measure costs that result from over-provisioning and under-provisioning [28]. Over-provisioning is a state when resources are available but are not used. Under-provisioning occurs when there is a higher demand of resources than are available. The costs for over-provisioning result from unused resources that must be paid for. Under-provisioning costs have their native in the users that stay absent due to the slow reaction of the system and thus not buying the offered products, for instance. While the costs for over-provisioning are clearly defined by the price model of the corresponding cloud provider, the costs for under-provision vary from the application domain and have to be researched empirically.

9.7 Dhrystone Benchmark

Dhrystone is a benchmark for the CPU performance like our MIPIPS benchmark and was originally developed by Weicker [74] in 1984. The first version was written in ADA and later translated to C. The name is an analogy to the Whetstone benchmark for floating point operations. In contrast, Dhrystone provides a measure of integer performance. Its output is the number of Dhrystones per second. Two versions of Dhrystone are available. These are 1.1 and 2.1. The second version tries to address the issue that optimizations of the compiler can be easily conducted and thus distorting the results.

Weicker gathered meta-data from a broad range of available software in 1984. The Dhrystone benchmark corresponds to a representative mix of instructions of the analyzed softwares. Therefore, Dhrystone is a synthetic benchmark.

9.8 Cloudstone Toolkit

Sobel et al. [59] developed the Cloudstone toolkit because they state that existing web benchmarking tools like SPECWeb are becoming less relevant in Web 2.0. The Cloudstone toolkit includes a multi-platform, multi-language benchmark, and measurement tools for Web 2.0. It has three components. The first component comprises of *Olio* [61] and *Faban* [14]. *Olio* consists of two implementations of a social-event calendar web application. These use Ruby on Rails and PHP, respectively. Both implementations feature user-generated content, social networking functions, and an AJAX-based user interface. *Faban* is an open source performance workload creation and execution framework. The second component is a set of automation tools for database population and metric gathering for testing *Olio*, for instance. A recommended methodology for calculation of the metric *dollars per user per month*, which was also developed by Sobel et al. [59], forms the third component.

10 Conclusions and Future Work

The remainder of this section concludes the main aspects of the thesis in Section 10.1 and describes the future work in Section 10.2.

10.1 Conclusions

During a cloud migration a cloud user has to assess a wide range of different cloud deployment options. For example, a selection of a cloud provider must be conducted. Furthermore, the mapping between services and virtual machine instances must be considered. The virtual machine instances' configuration and adaptation strategies must be also specified. Rewriting and testing the software with the different cloud deployment options is infeasible. Simulating the different deployment options assists to find the best ratio between high performance and low costs.

The thesis showed how cloud deployment options can be simulated. First, the diverse inputs and outputs of the simulation were described. Thus, accomplishing the goals G1 and G2. Three approaches for instruction count derivation and an approach for derivation of MIPIPS, a new measure for the computing performance of nodes, were developed. Furthermore, an approach for the derivation of the size of data types was described. Afterwards, the CloudSim enhancements, the MIPIPS and weights benchmark, and CDOSim were described which corresponds to the goals G3 and G4. The evaluation showed that CDOSim's simulation results are reasonable near to the conducted runs concerning accruing costs and performance. Especially, we demonstrated that CDOSim can sufficiently accurate predict the execution on a different cloud provider. Furthermore, the evaluation revealed that the performance on our Eucalyptus deployment decreases when more CPU cores are allocated and that the performance of *m1.small* instances on Amazon EC2 strongly varies.

10.2 Future Work

Most future work lies in enhancing and addition of features to CDOSim. In order to perform automatic optimization of cloud deployment options efficiently, it should be possible that simulations can run in parallel. However, CloudSim does not enable parallel simulations. Hence, CloudSim should be changed to support parallel simulations.

The conducted evaluations solely used the JPetStore application. Further evaluations with programs written in other programming languages should be carried out to see if the simulation works with these programs, too.

The static approach should be further enhanced with data flow analysis. The evaluation showed that the hybrid mode performs not as well as expected. However, it is the only reasonable approach when the separate submethod modeling mode is enabled. Hence, future work is to enhance the hybrid mode.

We derived the type size count by static counting. This should be improved by using dynamic analyses that log the size of the passed parameters in method invocations.

To give a quick overview of the simulation run, the run should be plotted on the GUI of CDOSim.

Considering elasticity as a further output can be useful for having a metric concerning the costs when resources are under-provisioned. This circumstance is only implicitly contained in the response times.

CDOSim lacks the feature to simulate availability zones and region concepts as for example used by Amazon EC2. In practice, these are important to make the software system, that shall be run in the cloud, more fault-tolerant to datacenter failures. Hence, availability zones and regions should be supported and a further desirable feature is to implement a way to simulate failures of datacenters.

Further adaptation strategies, especially cost-aware strategies, should be implemented because the current utilization-based adaptation strategy simply terminates an instance after, e.g., 60 seconds. In Amazon EC2, the virtual machine instance price is paid for full hours. Thus, the adaption strategy should wait until minute 59 passed and only then terminate the virtual machine instance.

References

[1] Jarmo Ahonen, Henna Sivula, Jussi Koskinen, Heikki Lintinen, Tero Tilus, Irja Kankaanpää, and Päivi Juutilainen. Defining the Process for Making Software System Modernization Decisions. In *Product-Focused Software Process Improvement*, volume 4034 of *Lecture Notes in Computer Science*, pages 5–18. Springer Berlin / Heidelberg, 2006. doi: 10.1007/11767718_5.

[2] Michael Armbrust, Armando Fox, Rean Griffith, Anthony D. Joseph, Randy H. Katz, Andrew Konwinski, Gunho Lee, David A. Patterson, Ariel Rabkin, Ion Stoica, and Matei Zaharia. Above the Clouds: A Berkeley View of Cloud Computing. Technical Report UCB/EECS-2009-28, EECS Department, University of California, Berkeley, February 2009.

[3] Steffen Becker, Heiko Koziolek, and Ralf Reussner. The palladio component model for model-driven performance prediction. *The Journal of Systems and Software*, 82:3–22, January 2009. doi: 10.1016/j.jss.2008.03.066.

[4] Anton Beloglazov and Rajkumar Buyya. Energy Efficient Allocation of Virtual Machines in Cloud Data Centers. pages 17–20, May 2010. doi: 10.1109/CCGRID.2010.45.

[5] Jean Bézivin, Grégoire Dupé, Frédéric Jouault, Gilles Pitette, and Jamal Eddine Rougui. First experiments with the ATL model transformation language: Transforming XSLT into XQuery. In *2nd OOPSLA Workshop on Generative Techniques in the context of Model Driven Architecture*, October 2003.

[6] Paul Brebner and Anna Liu. Modeling Cloud Cost and Performance. In *Cloud Computing and Virtualization (CCV 2010)*, pages 79–86, Singapore, May 2010.

[7] Rajkumar Buyya, Rajiv Ranjan, and Rodrigo N. Calheiros. Modeling and Simulation of Scalable Cloud Computing Environments and the CloudSim Toolkit: Challenges and Opportunities. IEEE Press, June 2009. doi: 10.1109/HPCSIM.2009.5192685.

[8] Rodrigo N. Calheiros, Rajkumar Buyya, and César A. F. De Rose. A Heuristic for Mapping Virtual Machines and Links in Emulation Testbeds. September 2009. doi: 10.1109/ICPP.2009.7.

[9] Rodrigo N. Calheiros, Rajiv Ranjan, César A. F. De Rose, and Rajkumar Buyya. CloudSim: A Novel Framework for Modeling and Simulation of Cloud Computing Infrastructures and Services. *CoRR*, abs/0903.2525, 2009.

[10] Rodrigo N. Calheiros, Rajiv Ranjan, Anton Beloglazov, César A. F. De Rose, and Rajkumar Buyya. CloudSim: a toolkit for modeling and simulation of cloud computing environments and evaluation of resource provisioning algorithms. *Software: Practice and Experience*, 41:23–50, January 2011. doi: 10.1002/spe.995.

[11] Andrea Camesi, Jarle Hulaas, and Walter Binder. Continuous Bytecode Instruction Counting for CPU Consumption Estimation. In *QEST 2006 (3rd International Conference on the Quantitative Evaluation of Systems*, pages 11–14. IEEE Computer Society, 2006.

[12] Chia-Chu Chiang and Coskun Bayrak. Legacy Software Modernization. In *SMC '06 IEEE International Conference on Systems, Man and Cybernetics*, volume 2, pages 1304–1309. IEEE Computer Society, October 2006. doi: 10.1109/ICSMC.2006.384895.

[13] Krzysztof Czarnecki and Simon Helsen. Classification of Model Transformation Approaches. In *OOPSLA 2003 Workshop on Generative Techniques in the Context of Model-Driven Architecture*, 2003.

[14] Faban. Faban. http://java.net/projects/faban/, last visited 2012-03-26.

[15] Sören Frey and Wilhelm Hasselbring. Model-Based Migration of Legacy Software Systems to Scalable and Resource-Efficient Cloud-Based Applications: The CloudMIG Approach. In *Proceedings of the First International Conference on Cloud Computing, GRIDs, and Virtualization (Cloud Computing 2010)*, pages 155–158, 2010.

[16] Sören Frey and Wilhelm Hasselbring. Model-Based Migration of Legacy Software Systems into the Cloud: The CloudMIG Approach. In *Proceedings of the 12th Workshop Software-Reengineering (WSR 2010)*, pages 59–60, 2010.

[17] Sören Frey and Wilhelm Hasselbring. An Extensible Architecture for Detecting Violations of a Cloud Environment's Constraints During Legacy Software System Migration. In *Proceedings of the 15th European Conference on Software*

Maintenance and Reengineering (CSMR 2011), pages 269–278, Oldenburg, Germany, March 2011. IEEE Computer Society. doi: 10.1109/CSMR.2011.33.

[18] Sören Frey and Wilhelm Hasselbring. The CloudMIG Approach: Model-Based Migration of Software Systems to Cloud-Optimized Applications. 2011. (to appear).

[19] Sören Frey, Wilhelm Hasselbring, and Benjamin Schnoor. Automatic Conformance Checking for Migrating Software Systems to Cloud Infrastructures and Platforms. *Journal of Software Maintenance and Evolution: Research and Practice*, 2012. doi: 10.1002/smr.582.

[20] Andy Georges, Dries Buytaert, and Lieven Eeckhout. Statistically rigorous java performance evaluation. *SIGPLAN Not.*, 42:57–76, October 2007. doi: 10.1145/1297105.1297033.

[21] Google. Google App Engine. `http://code.google.com/intl/de-DE/appengine/`, last visited 2012-03-26.

[22] Object Management Group. Knowledge Discovery Meta-Model v1.3. `http://www.omg.org/spec/KDM/1.3/`, last visited 2012-03-26.

[23] Object Management Group. Meta Object Facility (MOF) 2.0 Query/View/Transformation v1.1. `http://www.omg.org/spec/QVT/1.1/`, last visited 2012-03-26.

[24] Object Management Group. Structured Metrics Meta-Model. `http://www.omg.org/spec/SMM/`, last visited 2012-03-26.

[25] John Grundy, Gerald Kaefer, Jacky Keong, and Anna Liu. Guest Editors' Introduction: Software Engineering for the Cloud. *IEEE Software*, 29:26–29, 2012. doi: 10.1109/MS.2012.31.

[26] Jarle Hulaas and Walter Binder. Program transformations for light-weight CPU accounting and control in the Java virtual machine. *Higher Order Symbol. Comput.*, 21:119–146, June 2008. doi: 10.1007/s10990-008-9026-4.

[27] iBATIS team. JPetstore. `http://archive.apache.org/dist/ibatis/binaries/ibatis.java/JPetStore-5.0.zip`, last visited 2012-03-26.

[28] J. Idziorek. Discrete event simulation model for analysis of horizontal scaling in the cloud computing model. In *Proceedings of the 2010 Winter Simulation Conference (WSC)*, pages 3004–3014, December 2010. doi: 10.1109/WSC.2010.5678994.

[29] A. Iosup, N. Yigitbasi, and D. Epema. On the Performance Variability of Production Cloud Services. In *11th IEEE/ACM International Symposium on Cluster, Cloud and Grid Computing (CCGrid 2011)*, pages 104–113, may 2011. doi: 10.1109/CCGrid.2011.22.

[30] Sadeka Islam, Kevin Lee, Alan Fekete, and Anna Liu. How A Consumer Can Measure Elasticity for Cloud Platforms. Technical Report 680, University of Sydney, August 2011.

[31] Javier Luis Cánovas Izquierdo and Jesus Molina. An Architecture-Driven Modernization Tool for Calculating Metrics. *IEEE Software*, 27:37–43, 2010. doi: 10.1109/MS.2010.61.

[32] Meena Jha and Piyush Maheshwari. Reusing Code for Modernization of Legacy Systems. In *Proceedings of the 13th IEEE International Workshop on Software Technology and Engineering Practice*, pages 102–114. IEEE Computer Society, 2005. doi: 10.1109/STEP.2005.21.

[33] Frédéric Jouault and Ivan Kurtev. On the Architectural Alignment of ATL and QVT. In *Proceedings of the 2006 ACM symposium on applied computing*, SAC '06, pages 1188–1195. ACM, 2006. doi: 10.1145/1141277.1141561.

[34] Frédéric Jouault, Freddy Allilaire, Jean Bézivin, Ivan Kurtev, and Patrick Valduriez. ATL: a QVT-like transformation language. In *Companion to the 21st ACM SIGPLAN symposium on object-oriented programming systems, languages, and applications*, OOPSLA '06, pages 719–720. ACM, 2006. doi: 10.1145/1176617.1176691.

[35] Frédéric Jouault, F. Allilaire, J. Bézivin, and Ivan Kurtev. ATL: A model transformation tool. *Science of computer programming*, 72:31–39, June 2008. doi: 10.1016/j.scico.2007.08.002.

[36] Kyong Hoon Kim, Anton Beloglazov, and Rajkumar Buyya. Power-aware Provisioning of Cloud Resources for Real-time Services. ACM, 2009. doi: 10.1145/1657120.1657121.

[37] Jack P. C. Kleijnen. Verification and validation of simulation models. *European Journal of Operational Research*, 82(1):145–162, April 1995.

[38] Jussi Koskinen, Jarmo J. Ahonen, Henna Sivula, Tero Tilus, Heikki Lintinen, and Irja Kankaanpää. Software Modernization Decision Criteria: An Empirical Study. In *Proceedings of the Ninth European Conference on Software Maintenance and Reengineering CSMR 2005*, pages 324–331. IEEE Computer Society, March 2005. doi: 10.1109/CSMR.2005.50.

[39] Michael Kuperberg. *Quantifying and Predicting the Influence of Execution Platform on Software Component Performance*. PhD thesis, Univeristy of Karlsruhe, Karlsruhe, 2010.

[40] Michael Kuperberg, Martin Krogmann, and Ralf Reussner. ByCounter: Portable Runtime Counting of Bytecode Instructions and Method Invocations. In *Proceedings of the 3rd International Workshop on Bytecode Semantics, Verification, Analysis and Transformation (ETAPS 2008, 11th European Joint Conferences on Theory and Practice of Software)*, 2008.

[41] F. Liu, J. Tong, J. Mao, R. B. Bohn, J. V. Messina, M. L. Badger, and D. M. Leaf. NIST Cloud Computing Reference Architecture. http://www.nist.gov/manuscript-publication-search.cfm?pub_id=909505, last visited 2012-03-26. NIST SP - 500-292.

[42] Peter Mell and Timothy Grance. The NIST Definition of Cloud Computing. http://csrc.nist.gov/publications/nistpubs/800-145/SP800-145.pdf. NIST SP - 800-145.

[43] Daniel A. Menasce and Virgilio A. F. Almeida. *Capacity Planning for Web Services: Metrics, Models, and Methods*. Prentice Hall International, September 2001.

[44] Tom Mens and Pieter Van Gorp. A Taxonomy of Model Transformation and its Application to Graph Transformation. http://win.ua.ac.be/~lore/refactoringProject/publications/Mens2004MtransTaxoGT.pdf, 2004. last visited 2012-03-26.

[45] Microsoft Corporation. Windows Azure Platform. http://www.windowsazure.com/en-us/, last visited 2012-03-26.

[46] John Murphy. Performance engineering for cloud computing. In Nigel Thomas, editor, *Computer Performance Engineering*, volume 6977 of *Lecture Notes in Computer Science*, pages 1–9. Springer Berlin / Heidelberg, 2011. doi: 10.1007/978-3-642-24749-1_1.

[47] A. Nuñez, G.G. Castane, J.L. Vazquez-Poletti, A.C. Caminero, J. Carretero, and I.M. Llorente. Design of a flexible and scalable hypervisor module for simulating cloud computing environments. In *2011 International Symposium on Performance Evaluation of Computer Telecommunication Systems (SPECTS)*, pages 265–270, June 2011.

[48] A. Nuñez, J. Vázquez-Poletti, A. Caminero, J. Carretero, and I. Llorente. Design of a new cloud computing simulation platform. In Beniamino Murgante, Osvaldo Gervasi, Andrés Iglesias, David Taniar, and Bernady Apduhan, editors, *Computational Science and Its Applications - ICCSA 2011*, volume 6784 of *Lecture Notes in Computer Science*, pages 582–593. Springer Berlin / Heidelberg, 2011. doi: 10.1007/978-3-642-21931-3_45.

[49] Alberto Nuñez, Javier Fernández, José Daniel García, Laura Prada, and Jesús Carretero. SIMCAN: a SIMulator framework for computer architectures and storage networks. In *SimuTools*, pages 73–81. ICST, 2008.

[50] Obeo. ATL - a model transformation technology. http://eclipse.org/atl/, last visited 2012-03-26.

[51] openArchitectureWare.org. openArchitectureWare. http://www.openarchitectureware.org/, last visited 2012-03-26.

[52] Simon Ostermann, Kassian Plankensteiner, Radu Prodan, and Thomas Fahringer. GroudSim: An Event-based Simulation Framework for Computational Grids and Clouds. In *CoreGRID/ERCIM Workshop on Grids, Clouds and P2P Computing*. Springer, August 2010.

[53] Ricardo Pérez-Castillo, Ignacio García-Rodríguez De Guzmán, and Mario Piattini. Implementing business process recovery patterns through QVT transformations. In *Proceedings of the Third international conference on Theory and practice of model transformations*, ICMT'10, pages 168–183. Springer-Verlag, 2010. doi: 10.1007/978-3-642-13688-7_12.

[54] Ricardo Pérez-Castillo, Ignacio García-Rodríguez de Guzmán, and Mario Piattini. Knowledge Discovery Metamodel-ISO/IEC 19506: A standard to modernize legacy systems. *Computer Standards and Interfaces*, 33(6):519–532, 2011. doi: 10.1016/j.csi.2011.02.007.

[55] Matthias Rohr, André van Hoorn, Wilhelm Hasselbring, Marco Lübcke, and Sergej Alekseev. Workload-intensity-sensitive timing behavior analysis for distributed multi-user software systems. In *1st Joint WOSP/SIPEW International Conference on Performance Engineering (WOSP/SIPEW 2010)*, pages 87–92. ACM, January 2010.

[56] Robert G. Sargent. Verification and validation of simulation models. In *Proceedings of the 30th conference on Winter simulation*, WSC '98, pages 121–130, Los Alamitos, CA, USA, 1998. IEEE Computer Society Press.

[57] A. Udaya Shankar. Discrete-Event Simulation. Department of Computer Science, University of Maryland, January 1991.

[58] S. Sindhu and Saswati Mukherjee. Efficient Task Scheduling Algorithms for Cloud Computing Environment. In *High Performance Architecture and Grid Computing*, volume 169 of *Communications in Computer and Information Science*, pages 79–83. Springer Berlin Heidelberg, 2011. doi: 10.1007/978-3-642-22577-2_11.

[59] Will Sobel, Shanti Subramanyam, Akara Sucharitakul, Jimmy Nguyen, Hubert Wong, Arthur Klepchukov, Sheetal Patil, O Fox, and David Patterson. Cloudstone: Multi-platform, multi-language benchmark and measurement tools for web 2.0. http://radlab.cs.berkeley.edu/w/upload/2/25/Cloudstone-Jul09.pdf, July 2009. Abstract Paper.

[60] M. Sudha and M. Monica. Investigation on Efficient Management of workflows in cloud computing Environment. *International Journal on Computer Science and Engineering (IJCSE)*, 2:1841–1845, 2010.

[61] Sun Microsystems Inc. and U.C. Berkeley RAD Lab. Olio. http://incubator.apache.org/olio/, last visited 2012-03-26.

[62] The Apache Software Foundation. ActiveMQ. http://activemq.apache.org/, last visited 2012-03-26.

[63] The Apache Software Foundation. JMeter. http://jakarta.apache.org/jmeter/, last visited 2012-03-26.

[64] The Apache Software Foundation. Tomcat. http://tomcat.apache.org/, last visited 2012-03-26.

[65] The Eclipse Foundation. Eclipse Modeling Framework Project (EMF). http://www.eclipse.org/modeling/emf/, last visited 2012-03-26.

[66] The Eclipse Foundation. Xpand. http://www.eclipse.org/modeling/m2t/?project=xpand, last visited 2012-03-26.

[67] The hsql Development Group. HSQLDB. http://www.hsqldb.org/, last visited 2012-03-26.

[68] Klaus G. Troitzsch. Validating simulation models. In *Proceedings of 18th European Simulation Multiconference on Networked Simulation and Simulation Networks, SCS Publishing House*, pages 265–270, 2004.

[69] Cor van Dijkum, Dorien DeTombe, and Etzel van Kuijk. Validation of simulation models. *J. Artificial Societies and Social Simulation*, 3(1), 2000.

[70] André van Hoorn, Matthias Rohr, Wilhelm Hasselbring, Jan Waller, Jens Ehlers, Sören Frey, and Dennis Kieselhorst. Continuous Monitoring of Software Services: Design and Application of the Kieker Framework. Technical Report 0921, 2009.

[71] André van Hoorn, Matthias Rohr, and Wilhelm Hasselbring. Generating probabilistic and intensity-varying workload for Web-based software systems. In Samuel Kounev, Ian Gorton, and Kai Sachs, editors, *Performance Evaluation — Metrics, Models and Benchmarks: Proceedings of the SPEC International Performance Evaluation Workshop 2008 (SIPEW '08)*, volume 5119 of *Lecture Notes in Computer Science*, pages 124–143. Springer, June 2008.

[72] Robert von Massow. Performance simulation of runtime reconfigurable software architectures. Diploma thesis, University Oldenburg, Oldenburg, April 2010.

[73] Robert von Massow, André van Hoorn, and Wilhelm Hasselbring. Performance simulation of runtime reconfigurable component-based software architectures.

In Ivica Crnkovic, Volker Gruhn, and Matthias Book, editors, *Software Architecture*, volume 6903 of *Lecture Notes in Computer Science*, pages 43–58. Springer Berlin / Heidelberg, 2011. doi: 10.1007/978-3-642-23798-0_5.

[74] Reinhold P. Weicker. Dhrystone: a synthetic systems programming benchmark. *Commun. ACM*, 27:1013–1030, October 1984. doi: 10.1145/358274.358283.

[75] Joe Weinman. Time is Money: The Value of "On-Demand". http://joeweinman.com/Resources/Joe_Weinman_Time_Is_Money.pdf, January 2011. last visited 2012-03-26.

[76] Vladimir Omar Calderón Yaksiè. J-RAF - The Java Resource Accounting Facility. Master's thesis, University of Geneva, June 2002.

[77] B. P. Zeigler. *Theory of Modelling and Simulation*. Krieger, Malabar, 1985.

Appendices

A Glossary

ADM
    architecture-driven modernization

ATL
    Atlas Transformation Language

CDOSim
    Cloud Deployment Options Simulator

CEM
    Cloud Environment Model

EMF
    Eclipse Modeling Framework

IaaS
    Infrastructure-as-a-Service

KDM
    Knowledge Discovery Meta-Model

MIPIPS
    mega integer plus instructions per second

MIPS
    mega instructions per second

MOF
    Meta Object Facility

MVC
    Model-View-Controller

NIST
    National Institute of Standards and Technology

OCL
　Object Constraint Language

OMG
　Object Management Group

PaaS
　Platform-as-a-Service

PCM
　Palladio Component Model

QVT
　Query/View/Transformation

S2M
　separate submethods mode

SaaS
　Software-as-a-Service

SMM
　Structured Metrics Meta-Model

UML
　Unified Modeling Language

XMI
　XML Metadata Interchange

B Ecore Model for MIPIPS and Weights Benchmark

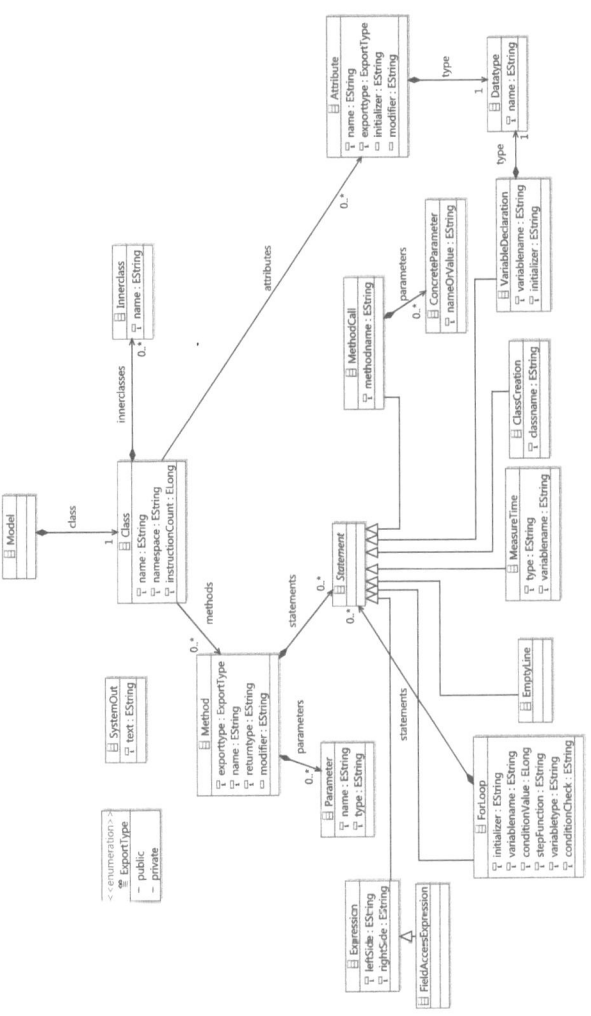

Figure 45: Ecore model for MIPIPS and weights benchmark as UML class diagram

C KDM example

```xml
<?xml version="1.0" encoding="ASCII"?>
<xmi:XMI xmi:version="2.0" xmlns:xmi="http://www.omg.org/XMI" xmlns:xsi
    ="http://www.w3.org/2001/XMLSchema-instance" xmlns:action="http://
    www.eclipse.org/MoDisco/kdm/action" xmlns:code="http://www.eclipse.
    org/MoDisco/kdm/code" xmlns:kdm="http://www.eclipse.org/MoDisco/kdm
    /kdm" xmlns:source="http://www.eclipse.org/MoDisco/kdm/source">
<kdm:Segment name="CloudMIGXpressTmpJavaProject1332585344928">
 <model xsi:type="code:CodeModel" name="Example">
  <codeElement xsi:type="code:Package" name="examplepackage">
   <codeElement xsi:type="code:ClassUnit" name="IfClass" isAbstract="
       false">
    <attribute tag="export" value="public"/>
    <source language="java">
     <region file="/0/@model.2/@inventoryElement.0" language="java"/>
    </source>
    <codeElement xsi:type="code:MethodUnit" name="main" type="/0/@model
        .0/@codeElement.0/@codeElement.0/@codeElement.0/@codeElement.0"
        >
     <attribute tag="export" value="public"/>
     <source language="java">
      <region file="/0/@model.2/@inventoryElement.0" language="java"/>
     </source>
     <codeElement xsi:type="code:Signature" name="main">
      <parameterUnit type="/0/@model.0/@codeElement.1/@codeElement.5"
          kind="return">
       <source language="java">
        <region language="java"/>
       </source>
      </parameterUnit>
      <parameterUnit name="args" type="/0/@model.1/@codeElement.1" kind
          ="unknown">
       <source language="java">
        <region file="/0/@model.2/@inventoryElement.0" language="java"/
            >
       </source>
      </parameterUnit>
     </codeElement>
     <codeElement xsi:type="action:BlockUnit">
      <source language="java">
```

```xml
30       <region file="/0/@model.2/@inventoryElement.0" language="java"/>
31      </source>
32      <codeElement xsi:type="action:ActionElement" name="variable
            declaration" kind="variable declaration">
33       <source language="java">
34        <region file="/0/@model.2/@inventoryElement.0" language="java"/
            >
35       </source>
36       <codeElement xsi:type="code:StorableUnit" name="i" type="/0/
            @model.0/@codeElement.1/@codeElement.0" kind="local">
37        <attribute tag="export" value="none"/>
38        <source language="java">
39         <region file="/0/@model.2/@inventoryElement.0" language="java"
            />
40        </source>
41        <codeRelation xsi:type="code:HasValue" to="/0/@model.1/
            @codeElement.2" from="/0/@model.0/@codeElement.0/
            @codeElement.0/@codeElement.0/@codeElement.1/@codeElement
            .0/@codeElement.0"/>
42       </codeElement>
43      </codeElement>
44      <codeElement xsi:type="action:ActionElement" name="if" kind="if">
45       <source language="java">
46        <region file="/0/@model.2/@inventoryElement.0" language="java"/
            >
47       </source>
48       <codeElement xsi:type="action:ActionElement" name="EQUALS" kind=
            "infix expression">
49        <source language="java">
50         <region file="/0/@model.2/@inventoryElement.0" language="java"
            />
51        </source>
52        <codeElement xsi:type="action:ActionElement" name="variable
            access" kind="variable access">
53         <actionRelation xsi:type="action:Reads" to="/0/@model.0/
            @codeElement.0/@codeElement.0/@codeElement.0/@codeElement
            .1/@codeElement.0/@codeElement.0" from="/0/@model.0/
            @codeElement.0/@codeElement.0/@codeElement.0/@codeElement
            .1/@codeElement.1/@codeElement.0"/>
54        </codeElement>
55        <codeElement xsi:type="code:Value" name="number literal" type="
            /0/@model.0/@codeElement.1/@codeElement.0" ext="5">
56         <source language="java">
```

```xml
                    <region file="/0/@model.2/@inventoryElement.0" language="java
                        "/>
                </source>
              </codeElement>
            </codeElement>
            <codeElement xsi:type="action:BlockUnit">
              <source language="java">
                <region file="/0/@model.2/@inventoryElement.0" language="java"
                    />
              </source>
              <codeElement xsi:type="action:ActionElement" name="expression
                  statement" kind="expression statement">
                <source language="java">
                  <region file="/0/@model.2/@inventoryElement.0" language="java
                      "/>
                </source>
                <codeElement xsi:type="action:ActionElement" name="ASSIGN"
                    kind="assignment">
                  <source language="java">
                    <region file="/0/@model.2/@inventoryElement.0" language="
                        java"/>
                  </source>
                  <codeElement xsi:type="code:Value" name="number literal" type
                      ="/0/@model.0/@codeElement.1/@codeElement.0" ext="3">
                    <source language="java">
                      <region file="/0/@model.2/@inventoryElement.0" language="
                          java"/>
                    </source>
                  </codeElement>
                  <actionRelation xsi:type="action:Writes" to="/0/@model.0/
                      @codeElement.0/@codeElement.0/@codeElement.0/@codeElement
                      .1/@codeElement.0/@codeElement.0" from="/0/@model.0/
                      @codeElement.0/@codeElement.0/@codeElement.0/@codeElement
                      .1/@codeElement.1/@codeElement.1/@codeElement.0/
                      @codeElement.0"/>
                </codeElement>
              </codeElement>
            </codeElement>
          </codeElement>
        </codeElement>
      </codeElement>
    </codeElement>
  </codeElement>
</codeElement>
```

```xml
 87   <codeElement xsi:type="code:LanguageUnit" name="Common Java datatypes
         ">
 88    <codeElement xsi:type="code:IntegerType" name="int"/>
 89    <codeElement xsi:type="code:IntegerType" name="long"/>
 90    <codeElement xsi:type="code:FloatType" name="float"/>
 91    <codeElement xsi:type="code:FloatType" name="double"/>
 92    <codeElement xsi:type="code:BooleanType" name="boolean"/>
 93    <codeElement xsi:type="code:VoidType" name="void"/>
 94    <codeElement xsi:type="code:CharType" name="char"/>
 95    <codeElement xsi:type="code:IntegerType" name="short"/>
 96    <codeElement xsi:type="code:OctetType" name="byte"/>
 97    <codeElement xsi:type="code:StringType" name="string"/>
 98   </codeElement>
 99  </model>
100  <model xsi:type="code:CodeModel" name="externals">
101   <codeElement xsi:type="code:Package" name="java">
102    <codeElement xsi:type="code:Package" name="lang">
103     <codeElement xsi:type="code:ClassUnit" name="String">
104      <source language="java">
105       <region language="java"/>
106      </source>
107      <codeRelation xsi:type="code:Implements" to="/0/@model.1/
             @codeElement.0/@codeElement.1/@codeElement.0" from="/0/@model
             .1/@codeElement.0/@codeElement.0/@codeElement.0"/>
108      <codeRelation xsi:type="code:Implements" to="/0/@model.1/
             @codeElement.0/@codeElement.0/@codeElement.1" from="/0/@model
             .1/@codeElement.0/@codeElement.0/@codeElement.0"/>
109      <codeRelation xsi:type="code:Implements" to="/0/@model.1/
             @codeElement.0/@codeElement.0/@codeElement.2" from="/0/@model
             .1/@codeElement.0/@codeElement.0/@codeElement.0"/>
110     </codeElement>
111     <codeElement xsi:type="code:TemplateUnit" name="Comparable&lt;T>">
112      <codeElement xsi:type="code:TemplateParameter" name="T"/>
113      <codeElement xsi:type="code:InterfaceUnit" name="Comparable">
114       <source language="java">
115        <region language="java"/>
116       </source>
117      </codeElement>
118     </codeElement>
119     <codeElement xsi:type="code:InterfaceUnit" name="CharSequence">
120      <source language="java">
121       <region language="java"/>
122      </source>
```

```xml
      </codeElement>
     </codeElement>
     <codeElement xsi:type="code:Package" name="io">
      <codeElement xsi:type="code:InterfaceUnit" name="Serializable">
       <source language="java">
        <region language="java"/>
       </source>
      </codeElement>
     </codeElement>
    </codeElement>
    <codeElement xsi:type="code:ArrayType" name="java.lang.String[]" size="1">
     <itemUnit type="/0/@model.1/@codeElement.0/@codeElement.0/@codeElement.0"/>
     <indexUnit type="/0/@model.0/@codeElement.1/@codeElement.0"/>
    </codeElement>
    <codeElement xsi:type="code:Value" name="number literal" type="/0/@model.0/@codeElement.1/@codeElement.0" ext="5">
     <source language="java">
      <region file="/0/@model.2/@inventoryElement.0" language="java"/>
     </source>
    </codeElement>
  </model>
  <model xsi:type="source:InventoryModel" name="source references">
   <inventoryElement xsi:type="source:SourceFile" name="IfClass.java" path="C:\Users\ffi\runtime-org.cloudmig.cloudmigxpress.product\Example\Source-Artifacts\Example\examplepackage\IfClass.java" language="java"/>
  </model>
  <model xsi:type="source:InventoryModel" name="CloudMIGXpressTmpJavaProject1332585344928">
   <inventoryElement xsi:type="source:Directory" name="CloudMIGXpressTmpJavaProject1332585344928" path="C:\Users\ffi\runtime-org.cloudmig.cloudmigxpress.product\CloudMIGXpressTmpJavaProject1332585344928">
    <inventoryElement xsi:type="source:Configuration" name=".classpath" path="C:\Users\ffi\runtime-org.cloudmig.cloudmigxpress.product\CloudMIGXpressTmpJavaProject1332585344928\.classpath"/>
    <inventoryElement xsi:type="source:Configuration" name=".project" path="C:\Users\ffi\runtime-org.cloudmig.cloudmigxpress.product\CloudMIGXpressTmpJavaProject1332585344928\.project"/>
    <inventoryElement xsi:type="source:Directory" name="bin" path="C:\Users\ffi\runtime-org.cloudmig.cloudmigxpress.product\
```

```
              CloudMIGXpressTmpJavaProject1332585344928\bin"/>
151      <inventoryElement xsi:type="source:Directory" name="lib" path="C:\
              Users\ffi\runtime-org.cloudmig.cloudmigxpress.product\
              CloudMIGXpressTmpJavaProject1332585344928\lib"/>
152      <inventoryElement xsi:type="source:Directory" name="src" path="C:\
              Users\ffi\runtime-org.cloudmig.cloudmigxpress.product\
              CloudMIGXpressTmpJavaProject1332585344928\src">
153        <inventoryElement xsi:type="source:Directory" name="main" path="C:\
              Users\ffi\runtime-org.cloudmig.cloudmigxpress.product\
              CloudMIGXpressTmpJavaProject1332585344928\src\main">
154          <inventoryElement xsi:type="source:Directory" name="examplepackage
              " path="C:\Users\ffi\runtime-org.cloudmig.cloudmigxpress.
              product\CloudMIGXpressTmpJavaProject1332585344928\src\main\
              examplepackage">
155            <inventoryElement xsi:type="source:SourceFile" name="IfClass.java
              " path="C:\Users\ffi\runtime-org.cloudmig.cloudmigxpress.
              product\CloudMIGXpressTmpJavaProject1332585344928\src\main\
              examplepackage\IfClass.java"/>
156          </inventoryElement>
157        </inventoryElement>
158        <inventoryElement xsi:type="source:Directory" name="misc" path="C:\
              Users\ffi\runtime-org.cloudmig.cloudmigxpress.product\
              CloudMIGXpressTmpJavaProject1332585344928\src\misc"/>
159      </inventoryElement>
160    </inventoryElement>
161  </model>
162 </kdm:Segment>
163 <kdm:Attribute tag="export" value="none"/>
164 </xmi:XMI>
165 }
```

Listing 20: Simple KDM example

D Rating Algorithm

```java
Map<Double, Double> rateValues(List<Double> values) {
  Map<Double, Double> resultList = new HashMap<Double, Double>();
  Collections.sort(values);

  double oneRatingValue = values.get(0);
  filterList(values, oneRatingValue);
  double threeRatingValue, fiveRatingValue = 0;

  resultList.put(oneRatingValue, 1.0);

  if (!values.isEmpty()) {
    int lastIndex = values.size() - 1;
    fiveRatingValue = values.get(lastIndex);
    filterList(values, fiveRatingValue);
    resultList.put(fiveRatingValue, 5.0);
  }

  if (!values.isEmpty()) {
    double median = median(values);
    threeRatingValue = median;

    if (values.contains(median)) {
      resultList.put(threeRatingValue, 3.0);
    }

    List<List<Double>> list = divideListWithoutMedian(values, median
        );

    workOnPartList(values, resultList, oneRatingValue,
      threeRatingValue, list.get(LEFT), 2.0);

    workOnPartList(values, resultList, threeRatingValue,
      fiveRatingValue, list.get(RIGHT), 4.0);
  }

  return resultList;
}

private void filterList(List<Double> values, double ratingValue) {
```

```java
39      List<Double> toRemove = new ArrayList<Double>();
40      for (Double value : values) {
41        if (doubleEqualsWithDelta(ratingValue, value)) {
42          toRemove.add(value);
43        }
44      }
45      for (Double toRem : toRemove) {
46        values.remove(toRem);
47      }
48    }
49
50    private boolean doubleEqualsWithDelta(double ratingValue, Double value) {
51      if (Double.compare(ratingValue, value) == 0) {
52        return true;
53      }
54      return Math.abs(value - ratingValue) <= 0.001;
55    }
56
57    private List<List<Double>> divideListWithoutMedian(List<Double> values, double median) {
58      List<Double> leftList = new Vector<Double>();
59      List<Double> rightList = new Vector<Double>();
60
61      for (Double value : values) {
62        if (value < median) {
63          leftList.add(value);
64        }
65        else if (value > median) {
66          rightList.add(value);
67        }
68        else {
69          // median is filtered
70        }
71      }
72
73      List<List<Double>> result = new Vector<List<Double>>();
74      result.add(leftList);
75      result.add(rightList);
76
77      return result;
78    }
79
```

```java
80    private void workOnPartList(List<Double> values, Map<Double, Double>
          resultList, double firstRatingValue, double thirdRatingValue,
         List<Double> srcList, double middleRank) {
81      if (!srcList.isEmpty()) {
82        double median = median(srcList);
83
84        if (values.contains(median)) {
85          resultList.put(median, middleRank);
86        }
87
88        List<List<Double>> list = divideListWithoutMedian(srcList,
             median);
89        List<Double> leftList = list.get(LEFT);
90        approximateLinearList(resultList, leftList, firstRatingValue,
             median, middleRank - 1.0);
91        List<Double> rightList = list.get(RIGHT);
92        approximateLinearList(resultList, rightList, median,
             thirdRatingValue, middleRank);
93      }
94    }
95
96    private void approximateLinearList(Map<Double, Double> resultList,
         List<Double> list, double leftRating, double rightRating, double
         rank) {
97      for (Double val : list) {
98        double rating = rank + approximateLinear(leftRating, rightRating
            , val);
99        resultList.put(val, rating);
100     }
101   }
102
103   private double approximateLinear(double leftGradeValue, double
         rightGradeValue, double value) {
104     double diff = rightGradeValue - leftGradeValue;
105     double diffValue = value - leftGradeValue;
106
107     return diffValue / diff;
108   }
```

Listing 21: Rating algorithm in Java

E Attachments

- One DVD labeled *Master's Thesis Attachment - Florian Fittkau* containing the source code for CDOSim and the MIPIPS and weights benchmark, created documents in PDF-format, used external test applications, and the monitored data for the conducted runs in the evaluations